Novice Language Teachers

Novice Language Teachers
Insights and Perspectives for the First Year

Edited by
Thomas S. C. Farrell

LONDON   OAKVILLE

Published by
Equinox Publishing Ltd
UK: Unit 6, The Village, 101 Amies St., London SW11 2JW
USA: DBBC, 28 Main Street, Oakville, CT 06779

www.equinoxpub.com

First published 2008

British Library Cataloguing-in-Publication Data

A catalogue record for this book is available from the British Library.

ISBN-13   978 1 84553 402 8   (hardback)
           978 1 84553 403 5   (paperback)

Library of Congress Cataloging-in-Publication Data

Novice language teachers: insights and perspectives for the first year/edited by Thomas S. C. Farrell.
    p. cm.
  Includes bibliographical references and index.
    ISBN-13: 978-1-84553-402-8 (hb)
    ISBN-13: 978-1-84553-403-5 (pb)
1. Language teachers—Training of. I. Farrell, Thomas S. C. (Thomas Sylvester Charles)
    P53.85.N68 2008
    418.007—dc22
                        2008004697

Typeset by S.J.I. Services, New Delhi
Printed and bound in Great Britain by Lightning Source UK Ltd, Milton Keynes

Contents

Contributors

Michaela Borg is a Learning and Development Adviser at the University of Warwick. She is interested in how people learn to teach; her current research is an investigation of doctoral students as they become acculturated into UK academic practice.

Lace Marie Brogden teaches in the Bac Program of the Faculty of Education, University of Regina, Canada. Her research interests include architecture and schooling, teacher induction, the negotiation of linguistic subjectivities of pre-service and in-service teachers, and writing as research.

Thomas S. C. Farrell is professor of Applied Linguistics at Brock University, Canada. His professional interests include Reflective Practice, and Language Teacher Education and Development. His recent most book is *Reflective Language Teaching: From Research to Practice* (2008, Continuum Press).

Alix Furness teaches in the English Language Institute at Bellevue Community College WA, USA.

David Hayes is Graduate Program Director, Department of Applied Linguistics, Brock University, Canada. His primary research interests are in the lives and careers of non-native speaking teachers of English in their own state educational systems and systemic educational change.

Yukie Iwamura is an instructor in the Academic English Program of Temple University, Japan Campus (TUJ). She is interested in teacher education and teaching academic English writing.

Steve Mann is Associate Professor at University of Warwick. He is particularly interested in teacher development, supporting teachers in action research projects, investigating professional interaction, and ESP course design and methodology.

Stephen Moore teaches in the Department of Linguistics at Macquarie University, Sydney. His research interests also include discourse analysis, TESOL teacher education, and language for specific purposes.

Becky Page, teaches in the North West Catholic School Division #16 Canada.

Martha C. Pennington is Professor of Writing and Linguistics at Georgia Southern University. Her scholarship encompasses the teaching of writing, phonology, applied linguistics, and English as a second language. Her most recent book is *Phonology in Context* (2007 Palgrave Macmillan).

Clea Schmidt is an Assistant Professor of Teaching English as an Additional Language at the University of Manitoba in Winnipeg, Canada. Her academic interests include the professional development of internationally educated teachers and EAL-inclusive teacher education.

Y. L. Teresa Ting teaches in the Faculty of Sciences, the University of Calabria, Italy. Integrating an MA-TEFL with a PhD in Neurobiology, she investigates EFL learning from a cognitive perspective, particularly, how constructivisitic science-content instruction motivates FL-learning.

Alan Urmston is Assistant Professor at the Hong Kong Polytechnic University. His professional interests include language assessment, language teacher education and ESL at tertiary level.

Michael Watts is a Senior Research Associate at the Von Hügel Institute, St Edmund's College, Cambridge. His recent research has focused on the ways in which students engage with the pedagogies they encounter in higher education in the UK.

1 Introduction: Insights and Perspectives for The First Year of Language Teaching

Thomas S. C. Farrell

Introduction

It has now been established that learning to teach is a complex process and that the first year of teaching has a very important impact on the future careers of beginning teachers (Bruckerhoff and Carlson, 1995; Featherstone, 1993; Solmon *et al.*, 1993). In fact, some educational researchers have called the first year for a teacher as a 'sink-or-swim experience' (Varah *et al.*, 1986). Although the first year of teaching has been well documented in general education research, (e.g. Bullough, 1989; Bullough, and Baughman, 1993; Calderhead, 1992), and even recently has been recognised by language teacher educators as having enormous influence on the future development of language teachers (e.g., Freeman and Johnson, 1998; Richards and Pennington, 1998), not many detailed studies outlining the experiences of language teachers in their first year of teaching have been documented in the second language education literature. This is surprising because as Freeman and Johnson (1998) have suggested, in order to establish an effective knowledge-base for language teacher education, teacher educators must have an understanding of schools and schooling and the social and cultural contexts in which learning how to teach takes place. Freeman and Johnson (1998) continue:

> Studying, understanding, and learning how to negotiate the
> dynamics of these powerful environments, in which some actions
> and ways of being are valued and encouraged whereas others are
> downplayed, ignored, and even silenced, is critical to constructing
> effective teacher education. (p. 409)

This edited volume on the first year of teaching language is a small attempt to fill the gap in the literature in language education by examining the various challenges and influences novice second language teachers in a variety of different contexts had to navigate when teaching during their first year.

The first year of teaching

The first year of teaching, defined in this collection as the period beyond the practicum (the first year) of transition that the novice teacher must make when moving from the teacher training institution to the school classroom to teach for the first time, has often been characterised as a type of 'reality shock' for many novice teachers (Veenman, 1984). This is because the ideals that the novice teacher formed during the teacher education programme are often replaced by the reality of classroom life in a new school culture. As Calderhead (1992) has pointed out, 'The novice [teacher] becomes socialized into a professional culture with certain goals, shared values and standards of conduct' (p. 6). This period of teacher socialisation during the first year is a 'learning process which requires developmental growth on the part of the novice teacher' (Bliss and Reck, 1991, p. 6). Early research by Fuller and Brown (1975) talked about a developing sequence of concerns that novice teachers face in their first year as they become socialised into the profession. For example, they describe two general stages of development for novice teachers. The first stage they say is characterised by survival and mastery while the second stage presents an either/or dichotomy of development: either settling into a state of resistance to change or staying open to adaptation and change of their practice. In the early stage of the first year of teaching there are early concerns about survival and this is more likely because the novice teacher's idealised concerns (the ideal of teaching before experiencing the reality of teaching) are replaced by concerns about his or her own survival as a teacher in the every-day classroom. At this stage novice teachers become very concerned about having full control of the class and the content of their instruction. In the later stage of the first year, teachers then become concerned about their own teaching performance, including the limitations and frustrations of the teaching situation. It is only much later (and probably not until the second year really) that Fuller and Brown (1975) suggest novice teachers become more concerned about their students' learning and the impact of their teaching on this learning.

Maynard and Furlong (1995, pp. 12–13) present a more detailed description of how novice teachers negotiate their first year. For instance, they suggest that novice teachers go through five stages of development as follows: (1) *early idealism*, (2) *survival*, (3) *recognising difficulties*, (4) *reaching a plateau*, and (5) *moving on*. *Early idealism* sees the novice teacher strongly identifying with their students but in contrast rejecting the image of what they perceive to be the older cynical teacher. The *survival* stage is where the novice teacher begins reacting to his or her perceived reality shock of the everyday classroom teaching situation and the growing feelings of being overwhelmed by the complexity of the teaching environment. The first year teacher really struggles to survive this complexity and Maynard and Furlong (1995) suggest that they try to get by with quick fix teaching and classroom management methods. The next stage of development, according to Maynard and Furlong (1995), is where the novice teacher begins to gain more of an awareness of his or her teaching situation and begins to really *recognise the difficulties* of not only the act of teaching but also that teachers (both novice and experienced) are limited in terms of what they can achieve. This in turn leads the novice teacher into the next stage where they enter a period a self-doubt where the novice really wonders if he or she will ever make it as a teacher. After overcoming the self-doubt, the first year teacher then enter a stage known as *reaching a plateau* where he or she starts to cope better with the routines of everyday teaching, but the teacher also develops a kind of resistance to trying any other new approaches or methods so as not to upset these newly developed (and perceived successful) routines. At this stage, the novice teacher becomes more focused on successful classroom management rather than on student learning. It is only much later, and possibly in the second and further years, that the novice teacher *moves on* and begins to focus on the quality of student learning in his or her class. Maynard and Furlong (1995) maintain that the novice teacher needs a lot of support at this stage or he or she will not be able to develop further as a result of possible burnout.

The experiences of second language teachers as they enter the teaching profession have been, as Richards and Pennington (1998) have pointed out, 'much less documented in the literature' (p. 173). Of the studies that do exist (with the exception of the 11 studies outlined in this volume), most address the transition from specific language teacher education courses to learning to teach on the practicum (e.g., Alamarza, 1996; Johnson, 1996; Pennington and Urmston, 1998; Richards *et al.*, 1996). Johnson's (1996) case study of how one novice teacher in a language teaching practicum attempted to endure difficulties in a real classroom, for example, highlighted the 'sink-or-swim' realities (Varah *et al.*, 1986) that many novice teachers experience during their first year and as a result of experiencing these difficult challenges, the novice teacher almost abandoned her plans to become a language teacher. At the time Johnson (1996) recognised a need for language teacher education programmes to be able to provide a more realistic view of classroom life so that the experience of becoming a language teacher would be 'less like "hazing" and more like professional development' (p. 48). Indeed Richards and Pennington's (1998) study of first year English language teachers in Hong Kong seemed to confirm Johnson's (1996) conclusion that language teacher education programmes are not preparing teachers adequately for their first year of teaching as the novice teachers in Hong Kong seemed to completely abandon or ignore many of the principles from their teacher education programme and they cited the novice teachers' preferences for 'familiar routines and practices' (p. 187) rather than try something they had learned in the teacher education programme. As a result of their findings, Richards and Pennington (1998) specifically proposed that teacher education should 'explicitly align itself with local practices or ... work to change those practices' (p. 190). However, more recently, Tarone and Allwright (2005) have unfortunately reached similar conclusions and have suggested that the differences between the academic course content in language teacher preparation programmes and the real conditions that novice teachers are faced with in the language classroom in their first year still appears to 'set up a gap that cannot be bridged by beginning teacher learners' (p. 12). This collection is nevertheless one attempt to bridge this gap and to eliminate some of the perceived 'hazing' effects of the first year of teaching by presenting eleven case studies of the experiences novice second language teachers during their first year of teaching.

This collection

As mentioned above, there are few studies on the actual experiences of novice language teachers in their first year, and given this paucity of research I hope this collection will provide more impetus for other language educators and novice language teachers to examine more closely what transpires during the first year of language teaching so we can build up a corpus of first year teaching studies from a variety of different settings and use these in language teacher education programmes.

These case studies can then be reflected on by preservice language teachers so that novice language teachers can be better prepared for the reality of what they will face in their first year of teaching. The topics covered in this edited collection cover such important issues such as *teacher socialisation, mentorship, stages of development, collegial support, classroom management, self-confidence,* and *professional identity and competence* of first year teachers. The collection also outlines the various methods of how data were collected that include narrative inquiry, story structure, introspection, case study, metaphor analysis, detailed interviews, and classroom observations. Except for this introductory chapter, and Chapters 10, 11 and 12 which are accounts of first year teacher experiences by the teachers themselves (although Chapter 10 is also coauthored with the researcher), for cohesive purposes each chapter (Chapter 2 to Chapter 9) is presented in the following format across these chapters: **Introduction** (what the focus of the chapter is about), **Literature review** (reviews the literature relevant to the particular focus of the first year experience), **Research methodology** (the methodology used in the study), **Findings** (outlines what occurred), **Discussion** (discusses the significance of the findings), and the **Conclusion**.

Chapter 2 by Steve Mann, *Teachers' use of metaphor in making sense of the first year of teaching,* uses metaphor analysis of several case studies that focus on how first-year teachers in the UK use metaphor to make sense of their first year of teaching. The findings suggest that the metaphors they used tended to be in the form of general comments (about the general nature of things rather than specifics of particular teaching interventions), and are also attempts these novice teachers make at encapsulating some general feelings about the teaching experiences. In terms of actual metaphors used, the study discovered that many of the metaphors were either about 'finding balance' (in the physical sense of keeping standing up, 'one hand and another' or 'finding feet') and that part of the challenge of the first year of teaching for many of the novice teachers was all about 'keeping some sense of balance.'

Chapter 3 by Steven Moore, *Trained for teaching high school, poached for teacher training: A case study of a Cambodian English teacher's first year of teaching in Cambodia,* outlines how a Cambodian teacher attempted to reconcile formal teacher training and actual classroom practice in her first year of language teaching. The teacher identified several key issues of importance for her in her first year of teaching that she grouped into two main sets: institutional and personal. Institutional issues that were important for her consisted of significant challenges concerned with: (1) the programme's transition from being taught by native English speakers to being taught by Cambodians; and (2) the programme's introduction of a student 'contribution' fee where previously students did not have to pay towards the cost of teaching materials and handouts. The novice teacher also identified four personal issues as being significant during her first year of teaching: (1) the pride and responsibility associated with being a university lecturer; (2) the issue of teaching classes in which as many as half the students had not done their homework; (3) the preparation necessary to deal with 'troublemakers'; and (4) the resistance of some students to the communicative teaching methodology used.

Chapter 4 by Thomas Farrell, *The First Year of Language Teaching: A Singapore Case Study*, outlines a case study of how a first year English language teacher in Singapore balanced a delicate, and sometimes conflicting, role between learning to teach and learning to become a teacher within an established school culture in Singapore. Using a story structure framework to help organise and analyse the data that followed a pattern of *setting – complication – resolution*, the findings suggest that the novice teacher faced three main complications during his first year: the teacher's learner-centred approach to teaching approach versus the established school teacher-centred approach, the required school curriculum versus the novice teacher's desired curriculum, and various complications related to collegial relations.

Chapter 5 by David Hayes, *Occupational socialization in the first year of teaching: perspectives from Thailand*, outlines a case study of how Thai teachers navigated their first year of teaching. This study utilised a life history research method that included detailed interviews and classroom observations to establish the teacher's identity within the institutional context of the school. The findings revealed that none of the four Thai teachers in this study experienced any formal process of induction beyond an initial meeting with the institution head, being introduced to fellow teachers by the head of department and an introduction to the student population during a school assembly. Thus learning institutional norms of behaviour is patently more difficult for beginning teachers within a culture of professional isolation than within a culture of collaboration. Similar to the findings in the previous chapter, the experiences of participants in this study indicate that more thorough preparation for all the roles that a teacher has to fulfil in school, as well as some guidance in dealing with the formal structures of schools as organisations and professional relationships with colleagues would alleviate some of the burdens that teachers face in their first year of teaching.

Chapter 6 by Clea Schmidt, *The Transition from Teacher Education to ESL/EFL Teaching in the First Year for Non-Native English Speaking Teachers in Canada*, documents non-native English speaking teacher (NNEST) participants' experiences beyond the certificate in teaching English to speakers of other languages (C-TESL) programme as they transitioned into their first year of language teaching. Using in-depth interviews with NNESTs and their C-TESL instructors, the results of this study reveal the participating NNESTs' concerns during their first year centred mainly on issues related to their self-confidence, their perceived professional competence, and experiences concerning discrimination in hiring practices that relate directly to language proficiency and concepts of language ownership. Although the study recognises continued support and encouragement provided for NNESTs with the framework of teacher education programmes, the results also suggest that language teacher educators explicitly challenge systemic barriers to the successful integration of NNESTs in the ESL teaching profession.

Chapter 7 by Alan Urmston and Martha Pennington, *The beliefs and practices of novice teachers in Hong Kong: change and resistance to change in an Asian teaching context*, outlines the experiences of new teachers in Hong Kong following their graduation by utilising interviews and lesson observations. Results indicate that the domination of examinations in the context of Hong Kong overly influenced the novice teachers' teaching approaches as they found it difficult to adopt interactive or innovative approaches. In addition, the novice teachers felt constrained by a need to follow a set syllabus and course textbook, a similar finding to Farrell's case study outlined in Chapter 5. One of the most noticeable aspects of the observations was the degree of inconsistency demonstrated by the teachers in terms of their stated beliefs and actually classroom practices during their first year of teaching.

Chapter 8 by Michela Borg, *Teaching Post-CELTA: the interplay of novice teacher, course and context*, outlines how native English speaking teachers who undertook a four week initial teacher training certificate (Certificate in English Teaching to Adults) in the UK and then went on to work in teaching English in a variety of settings in Europe. Results show that all the participating teachers faced various challenges in their first year of teaching, and these challenges came mainly from the different contexts in which they found themselves teaching.

While other chapters in this volume address first year teacher experiences in the teaching English as a subsequent language (TESL) context,

Chapter 9, by Lace Brogden and Becky Page, *Ghosts on the cupboard: language/lessons and other discursive hauntings during the first year of teaching French Immersion in Canada*, provide examples from another language environment, specifically French Immersion in Canada, and reports on the ongoing struggle that was present in the difference between what a first year teacher of French language felt was expected of her, and what she implemented in her classroom during her first year. This study highlights among other issues, the role mentorship can and should play in contributing to a positive induction experience of a first year teacher.

Chapter 10 by Teresa Ting and Michael Watts, *From rats to language learners: The transition from the biochemistry laboratory to the language classroom in the First year of teaching*, outlines how the authors use narrative inquiry and co-narrate their story of the metamorphosis of a biochemist into a first year EFL (English as a foreign language) teacher in Italy. In this chapter, it is the language teacher who is the researcher and the mentor (second author) the guide. It is an example of how, equipped with suitable *professional tools*, a teacher can assume the role of teacher-*researcher* to generate field-based insights for fellow novice teachers. The reader is invited to read this 'professional transition story' as a first step towards your own professional development, identifying for your own idiosyncratic context, aspects of this unusual transition which can best facilitate your own entrance into the FL classroom. Among other findings this chapter outlines how, in the absence of collegial support, Teresa (the first year teacher) engaged with her new-found community of practice through journal articles which initially enabled her to share in communal repertoire and subsequently guided her contributions to the joint enterprise of defining 'good' EFL practices. This invaluable 'research attitude', instilled upon her during her biochemist-training, buoyed Teresa through her *survival stage* (see above for a discussion on the stages of first year teacher development) during her first year as an EFL teacher.

Chapter 11 by Alix Furness, *Formation of ESL teacher identity during the first year: an introspective study*, and as the title suggests, is an introspective study of how the author analysed her teaching journals written during the first year of teaching in two junior high schools in Japan. The most prominent themes and patterns that emerged from these journal entries included the several stages of development this first year teacher experienced included such issues as wanting to define purpose and role in the school, feelings of exclusion, nervousness, passivity, boredom and frustration, the development of relationships with students and colleagues, and ultimately gaining confidence.

Chapter 12 by Yukie Iwamura, *The first year of language teaching in Japan*, is a first person narrative account of her first years of teaching and in particular, two major transitions she made. The first transition took place when she became a public junior high school teacher after graduating from a university in Japan; the second was when she started to teach preschool and elementary school children at a private English conversation school. During each transition as a novice teacher she was faced with many different challenges and this chapter outlines how reflection helps her predict problems she may face for her third and current transition as she currently becomes a university teacher.

Conclusion

The examples of first year language teacher research presented in this volume offer a small window into the different worlds of novice second language teachers as they move between different stages of socialisation and development during their first year. Much more research needs to be conducted on the experiences of novice second language teachers during their first year of teaching in order for teacher education courses to be better able to prepare these them for the transition from the language teacher education programme to the reality of the classroom.

References

Bliss, L. B., and Reck, U. M. (1991). *PROFILE: An Instrument for Gathering Data in Teacher Socialization Studies* (ERIC Document Reproduction Service No. 330 662).

Bruckerhoff, C. E., and Carlson, J. L. (1995). Loneliness, fear and disrepute: The haphazard socialization of a student teacher. *Journal of Curriculum Studies,* 24, 431–44.

Bullough, R. V. (1989). *First Year Teacher: a Case Study*. New York: Teachers College Press.

Bullough, R. V. and Baughman, K. (1993). Continuity and change in teacher development: a first year teacher after five years. *Journal of Teacher Education,* 44, 86–95.

Calderhead, J. (1992). Induction: a research perspective on the professional growth of the newly qualified teacher. In *The Induction of Newly Appointed*

Teachers, General Teaching for England and Wales. London: General Teaching Council, 5–21.

Carew, J., and Lightfoot, S. L. (1979). *Beyond Bias: Perspectives on Classrooms*. Cambridge, MA: Harvard University Press.

Featherstone, H. (1993). Learning from the first years of classroom teaching: The journey in, the journey out. *Teacher's College Record, 95*, 93–112.

Freeman, D., and Johnson, K. E. (1998). Reconceptualizing the knowledge-base of language teacher education. *TESOL Quarterly, 32*, 397–417.

Fuller, F. F. and Brown, O. H. (1975). Becoming a teacher. In K. Ryan (Ed.), *Teacher Education: The Seventy-fourth Yearbook of the National Society for the Study of Education* (pp. 25–51). Chicago, IL: National Society for the Study of Education.

Johnson, K. E (1992). Learning to teach: instructional actions and decisions of preservice ESL teachers. *TESOL Quarterly, 26*, 507–35.

Johnson, K. E. (1996). The vision versus the reality: The tensions of the TESOL practicum. In D. Freeman and J. Richards (Eds), *Teacher Learning in Language Teaching* (pp. 30–49). New York: Cambridge University Press.

Maynard, T. and Furlong, J. (1995). Learning to teach and models of mentoring, In T. Kelly and A. Mayes (Eds). *Issues in Mentoring* (pp. 10–30). London: Routledge.

Pennington, M. and Urmston, A. (1998). The teaching orientation of graduating students on a BATESL course in Hong Kong: a comparison with first-year students. *Hong Kong Journal of Applied Linguistics, 3* (2), 17–45.

Richards, J. C. and Pennington, M. (1998). The first year of teaching. In J. C. Richards (Ed.) *Beyond Training,* (pp. 173–90). New York: Cambridge University Press.

Richards, J. C., Ho, B. and Giblin, K. (1996). Learning how to teaching in the RSA Cert. In D. Freeman and J. C. Richards (eds), *Teacher Learning in Language Teaching,* (pp. 242–59). New York: Cambridge University Press.

Solmon, M. A., Worthy, T. and Carter, J. A. (1993). The interaction of school context and role identity of first-year teachers. *Journal of Teaching in Physical Education, 12*, 313–28.

Tarone, E and Allwright, D. (2005). Second language teacher learning and student second language learning: shaping the knowledge Base. In D. J. Tedick (Ed.), *Second Language Teacher Education* (pp. 5–23). Mahwah, NJ: Lawrence Erlbaum.

Varah, L. J., Theune, W. S. and Parker, L. (1986). Beginning teachers: sink or swim? *Journal of Teacher Education, 37,* 30–3.

Veenman, S. (1984). Perceived problems of beginning teachers. *Review of Educational Research, 54,* 143–78.

2   Teachers' use of metaphor in making sense of the first year of teaching

Steve Mann

Introduction

This chapter describes how the process of metaphorical articulation may be an important part of coming to terms with the first year of teaching and helping a teacher move on. Five case studies focus on how first-year teachers use metaphor to make sense of the beginning of their teaching career. The chapter will consider how they vary in metaphor use and in the degree to which 'core metaphors', established in the teacher education programme, remain relevant or are reshaped by their teaching context. The chapter also considers some common features of the metaphors that emerge and makes some more general points about the relationship between reflection and metaphor use in the first year. This chapter is also interested in the relationship between opportunities for reflecting through metaphor on a teacher education programme and whether these metaphorical reflections play an important heuristic role. If the first year of teaching is difficult, then we should be able to see evidence of problems being constructed and articulated through metaphor in order to make sense of troubling situations.

Background Literature

Lakoff and Johnson (1980) have been particularly influential in the development of our appreciation of the important and pervasive ways in which metaphors shape our ideas and our lives. Metaphors play an instrumental role in using a familiar image to explore more complex concepts or meaning. They are an integral part of our understanding and action (Taylor 1985). Schon (1983) first argued that metaphorical exploration provides useful insights and reflection points for individual teachers and that metaphors are central to the creation of new perceptions and understandings. Metaphor can be consciously employed by individuals for reflective purposes. They are used as 'explanatory vehicles' (Block 1996: 51–3) or useful tools to enable teachers to reflect, analyse, evaluate, and restructure their practice (Zuzovsky 1994). Individuals use metaphor construction as an 'introspective and reflective tool … tapping the kinds of meanings practitioners create about their own professional actions, practices and personal theories' (Burns 1999: 147). The exploration of ideas through metaphor is an integral part of reflective practitioner thought and, as Oxford *et al.* state, such thought and reflection is 'part of the ongoing life of each language teacher' (1998: 46).

Although it is recognised that metaphorical reflection is essentially an individual tool, there have been a number of papers that have argued for such reflection to be incorporated within the teacher education process. It has been argued that metaphors used may be revealing of beliefs and this is why they are particularly interesting for teacher educators (Bullough and Knowles 1991; Bullough and Stokes 1994; Tobin 1990). Munby argued that it may be profitable to attend to the metaphors used by teachers (1986) and Thornbury (1991: 193) sees the beliefs and values embodied in 'personally significant images' as providing 'valuable insights for teacher educators'. Farrell (2006a) demonstrates the role of metaphor in revealing existing beliefs and theories before, during and after teaching practice. Whilst it has been argued that individuals can use metaphor in a conscious exploratory way, much of the teacher education literature looks at metaphor being used below the level of awareness (e.g. Clark and Peterson 1986) and teacher education can help 'free' teachers from tacit images (Roberts 1998; Thornbury 1991). It has been pointed out that students are more likely to accept information and practices that fit with their beliefs and ignore those that contradict them (Zeichner *et al.* 1987) and so metaphors can be helpful in assessing what new information may be helpful for an individual teacher.

Metaphorical exploration may be particularly helpful for first year teachers in attempting to come to terms with the complex nature of teacher knowledge and its relationship with experience. It is now well recognised that an individual teacher is constantly reshaping knowledge and that new understanding 'emerges from a process of reshaping existing knowledge, beliefs, and practices' (Johnson and Golombek 2003). Resolving the complex interplay between declarative or received knowledge, on the one hand, and personal, experiential and local knowledge (e.g. Wallace 1991) may mean that metaphorical articulation is particularly helpful in reflective teacher development.

There have been studies which have concentrated on 'root metaphors' (Massengil *et al.* 2005; Oxford *et al.* 1998) and Massengil *et al.* suggest that metaphorical constructs are persistent. This paper considers the possibility that metaphors help to articulate emergent understandings. Mann (2003) argues that individuals often use metaphor as specific points of comparison in a formative process of articulation. Such metaphor use is therefore relatively temporary and acts as a dialogic catalyst for further articulation. It is dialogic because there is a 'conversation' between the adopted metaphor and the target emergent meaning. Hence metaphor use prompts confirmation, clarification, modification, extension, and shifts in understanding. An important element of this chapter is therefore to look for both evidence of the persistence of root metaphors and evidence of more transient metaphor use.

Research methodology

Context

The students featured in the case study presented in this chapter had recently completed an MA Education TEFL programme in the School of Education at University of Birmingham, UK. Some of the students on this programme have teaching experience but those featured here had no previous experience and are in their 'first year'. Although there is contextual detail concerning these teachers' first-year teaching contexts, it is worth making a few comments on the rationale and nature of this programme. This is because this chapter is explicitly concerned with the relationship between root-metaphors elicited on the MA programme and their first year experience. The programme is also likely to be a factor in teachers' attitudes to making space for reflective thought. It is also a strong possibility that the content and methodology of this programme may have influenced the nature of teacher expectations, knowledge, and attitudes to learning and perhaps the metaphors through which aspect of teaching and learning are explored.

The programme stresses the following themes:

- Appropriate methodology (Holliday 1994) and the importance of developing an individual sense of plausibility (Prabhu 1991).

- Loop learning (Woodward 1991). As much as possible, explicit links are encouraged between students' experience on the teacher education programme and language learners'.

- Opportunities for observation of language teaching and the integration of opportunities for micro-teaching.

- Action research (Burns 2005) – a view of research as potentially led by teacher practitioners.

- Reflective practice – students are provided with examples of techniques and ideas for individual and collaborative reflection, including reflective journals.

- Exploring digital technology both as a tool for teacher development, practitioner research and language learning. This includes blogging, e-mail, discussion lists, Skype and web design.

- Balancing opportunities for self-evaluation, peer-evaluation and tutor-evaluation (Mann 2004).

- Importance of peer collaboration (Burns 1999) cooperative development (Edge 1992, 2002) the role of the critical friend (Farrell 2001).

It will be evident from this list of priorities that this MA programme is typical of many in Language Teacher Education where there has been a movement away from transmission of products to a more 'constructivist, process orientated' views of learning and education (Crandall 2000: 34).

Early in the programme students are encouraged to arrive at a personal metaphor. A series of related prompts are used (*the teacher is …. the classroom is …, the learning process is … and the learner is …*). Later in the programme students revisit their original metaphors and see if they want to modify, change, add detail, etc. This process is exploratory and intended to promote 'dialogic understanding' (Mann 2003). The programme consciously attempts to respond to Bullough's (1991) plea for more space for teachers to explore their personal constructs rather simply impose new ones.

Methodology

This study is best conceptualised as a case study within an ongoing series of action research cycles concerned with encouraging reflective practice (Mann 2005). Although the longer term action research process draws on a combination of ethnographic observations, interviews, and content analysis, this particular case study relies on the content analysis of e-mails exchanged with the researcher. There is also some similarity between the methodology adopted in this case study and a narrative case study approach (Kelchtermans 1994, 1999) designed to collect instances of reflective writing.

In terms of fulfilling the criteria for 'specificity or boundedness' outlined by Stake (2000: 436) for qualitative case studies, the five 'cases' share the same MA TEFL programme and also having to negotiate a first year of language teaching together. However, there are also important and inevitable differences in teaching context in the sample that need to be detailed and taken into account. In terms of Merriam's (1998) summary of the special qualities of a case study, this study is 'particularistic' in that it focuses on a particular phenomenon (metaphor use in reflective writing), 'descriptive' in that it provides rich description of instances of the phenomenon, and 'heuristic' in that it is written with the view of enhancing readers' understanding of the phenomenon.

It is worth clarifying how this focus on metaphorical reflection developed. The impetus for keeping in touch with students was initially to collect a series of critical incidents and perspectives. It was explained that such 'critical incidents' would not necessarily be large-scale or 'extreme' but could be would likely be 'a commonplace, everyday event or interaction, but they would be `critical' in that it stands out for you' (Kenn 1996: 2). So, although it was an explicit aim of the actual MA programme to encourage metaphorical exploration this first-year phase of exchanging e-mails was not initially or explicitly to encourage metaphor use. It was only once I began to read the e-mails that this research focus emerged. In fact, prior permission was sought to use 'incidents' within the MA Education programme with future students as discussion texts. In terms of the ethical warrant, it was only after the vignettes had been completed that these were validated as accurate representations and that permission was sought for use reporting metaphor use. In an important sense then the metaphor use was not 'encouraged' and the research process as naturalistic as possible. In my responses I tried not to foreground the issue of metaphor use, as there was a danger that metaphors might be used for show and perhaps forced in some way. It could still be argued that the teachers have somehow been encultured into greater metaphor use. However, there is always going to be some kind of reflexive relationship between a teacher education programme and the first year.

Initially 11 students were invited to keep some sort of reflective journal. Out of a larger MA group (N19), these were the only ones that I knew had secured teaching posts. The five featured in this study varied in when their first year commenced. Two started in September 2005, one November 2005 and two in January 2006. These five were the only ones able to maintain any meaningful contact with the researcher and it was a conscious decision not to put any undue pressure on any of the other teachers. The five all reported later that keeping in contact had been helpful. Although the only texts featured here are from e-mails these texts have an obvious relationship with reflective journals the five reportedly kept. It is obvious from their descriptions that the amount they write varies considerably. Sometimes they 'quote' from the journal text and sometimes it is more difficult to tell if they writing/reflecting in real-time. As there are difficulties in determining this relationship, the researcher makes no attempt to differentiate. Rather, they are both treated as 'reflective writing'.

Findings

Case study vignettes

The remainder of this chapter presents six vignettes. Each vignette presents details of the individual language teacher's first-year experience, including relevant details of their teaching context. The starting point is a summary of their root metaphor elicited during the MA TEFL programme. Pseudonyms are used as anonymity was assured.

John

John started out the MA programme with a relatively optimistic root metaphor of 'shepherd', although later in the programme he revisited this metaphor and substituted it with 'train conductor'. John has been teaching in a private language institution in Taiwan. Despite being in his first year, he has been asked to take further responsibility ('Head of School English Department') in his primary school because 'he is the only one with a TEFL MA'. It is clear from his e-mails that his role dealing with other staff greatly adds to his stress levels. When he is not teaching he is 'working in teams on developing the school English curriculum'. He uses the metaphor 'coaching a team' several times for this aspect of his work. One of the difficult aspects of his role is 'how to communicate well with other English teachers from different countries and background' in developing a new Curriculum. He is clearly concerned with identity and relationships both in terms of power and having to 'act':

> It is difficult to be a 'Boss' and to order people do[1] something
> when I am younger. I always try to be nice to people and be calm
> but I need to use some power at the same time. Well, this is not
> my style. I think I am becoming a good actor, ha ha!

In terms of his actual teaching, he is a 'class tutor' and has 'to teach three classes English language'. He is concerned with control and discipline and twice uses the metaphor 'policeman':

> To look after 96 kids in the three classes, I have to be a Policeman.
> Lately the boys in my tutor class are so naughty. I am tired when I
> go home.

Although further e-mails report improvement ('beginning to know the individuals' and 'getting to know individual personality') problems persist. In one lengthy e-mail detailing various difficulties he refers to the job as being 'a custodial officer' where he is 'running a prison'. As Spencer says, 'teachers find that real children in real classrooms are not always lovable …'(1986: 10). It is the growing realisation that rules are not being followed that encourages this metaphor. Students 'are not following the rules … not showing respect … hindering other pupils … going to toilet without permission'. It is a long list. A later e-mail suggests progress as begins to engage with parents 'helping to support the students to learn' and as the parents get involved the students become more motivated. There is little evidence of his root metaphor. Perhaps the closest he gets is talking about 'individual pastoral care' and 'leading individual students once I know the individual problem and family background and how to help'.

Izumi

Izumi's root metaphor on the MA was a 'marketing researcher' who 'can figure out what is needed and supply products'. Izumi showed a great deal of interest in Task Based Learning and her dissertation investigated interaction in a variety of task types. This is significant because her commitment to CLT and TBL as a teacher seems later to cause conflict. She is now an English language teacher in a private Senior High School in Japan.

In the early e-mails there is some evidence that Izumi's root metaphor has been sustained, although the root metaphor is not used explicitly. She calls students and parents 'difficult customers' who are 'hard to please'. There is certainly an implicit sense of conflict between her 'product' (CLT methodology) and student (customer) expectations. In terms of explicit difficulties, she feels that she is compared unfavourably with other teachers:

> My students have 'high expectation' and told me that they
> compare me to last year's teacher. This causes feeling strong
> pressure comparing me as a new teacher with the experienced
> senior teacher.

However, there is evidence from her first year that she has shifted to seeing the classroom as less of a learning environment and more of a 'manager' or 'controller'. There is a continuing and marked frustration evident in the conflict between her desire to introduce CLT/TBL and students' perceived needs. Although anticipated, she is surprised by the impact of the university entrance examinations as they exert a strong 'washback' effect. This becomes a customer satisfaction issue as 'two classes insist on translation sentences from Japanese to English in class' and 'some parents ask for more of this too'. It is clear that this need is not one that Izumi feels committed to:

> However, people do not really have to translate so much in daily
> life. Parents have a different educational concepts compared with
> my teaching style.

It seems that the root metaphor has been weakened by her commitment to at least some communicative principles. She does not feel comfortable simply supplying what is felt to be 'needed'. Indeed later e-mails report persistent attempts at 'trying to introduce some more CLT activities' despite 'resistance from some students' who perceive the CLT product as 'a waste of time'. Bad feeling with students persists and they report to her that 'they do not want to waste their time to be the experimented objects of the new teacher'. As she begins to doubt her ability to satisfy the class, the 'way has become dark' and 'it is difficult to know which way to go now'. She also finds it 'difficult to put herself in her students' shoes' and 'to understand why they are not studying. It becomes a 'struggle to move forward'. She refers to herself as 'a horse' working very hard to get things done 'pulling the students forward without resting'.

Tom

Tom started the MA with a root metaphor of 'ship captain'. This was confirmed as his preferred metaphor later in the MA programme. However he said that it helps if the captain also has 'engineering skills'. He thought that a combination of good leadership and being able to 'fix things on the spot' was important. He is now teaching in a primary school in Cyprus.

There are two main themes in Tom's e-mails. He is very concerned with 'getting the right amount of time for each activity' and 'keeping a balance' is a much used phrase. This is a typical comment:

> What I have difficulty in balancing in my teaching is how many times and what amount of time must I spend on a particular thing (grammar, vocabulary etc.) if I think the students, or at least some students do not understand. But I am slowly finding my feet.

Although there are no instances of his 'root' metaphor being used explicitly, it is possible that there may be a link between the idea of sailing and stormy weather. This is evident in one phrase 'keeping the boat afloat'. Certainly coping with difficult weather conditions is very evident as a metaphor. There are two e-mails where his relationship with a class is described as 'stormy' and one instance of 'keeping on my feet in a hurricane'. On another occasions he equates the job with 'trying to build a house in strong winds'. In another he is 'an acrobat performing difficult routines' and in another 'a tight-rope act walking in the wind'. He also uses metaphors of construction, house building and decorating. It is interesting that Tom added 'engineer' to his root metaphor because there is evidence of some metaphorical threads – 'applying jump leads' 'student's short circuiting' 'this last lesson the wheels really came off'. Perhaps not being able to fix things easily, Tom's e-mails uses metaphors of control consistent with Oxford's 'social control' classification (1998: 7) and twice refers to being a 'policeman'. It may be that the original commanding metaphor of 'Captain' has been replaced, as he is pulled in various directions by forces difficult to control:

> There is mixed direction … so on the one hand is the inspector who demands all these and the other hand is the problem I find when I put the ideas into practice.

These problems can be severe at times. Any kind of communicative games or pair work cause problems and 'especially role play in the classroom usually ends in a chaos'. There is a feeling of lack of lack of experience and a need for 'more experience in order to face them'. The inspector 'demands the implementation of the communicative approach' and 'maybe she doesn't realize that it cannot be implemented in all classes because some children may be unable to follow'. Trying to keep a happy medium between play and learning is clearly an issue:

> What I mean is that children misunderstand the meaning of
> playing games during a lesson period and they think that now is
> time to play only and not play and learn simultaneously. These are
> my main concerns for the moment.

Connie

Connie's root metaphor of a 'farmer' who is 'engaged in growing vegetables' remained intact during the MA stage of this research. Although it seems to be a metaphor that sees the farmer as essentially horticultural; where the classroom is a greenhouse for 'growing up plants'. Connie began work in a kindergarten but quickly switched to a post in a private secondary school in Shanghai.

Data collected during her first year sees a continued use of metaphor connected to growth. In this example she is talking about selecting appropriate vocabulary to concentrate on:

> Which vocabulary to choose is like seeds in the ground ... too
> many growing and maybe they all don't grow ... it is better to pick
> out some to get stronger ... then keep going back, watering and
> feeding ... replanting, then they are more likely to make it.

In another e-mail Connie is talking about her relative success with one group:

> Teachers are gardeners who take the responsibility for planting
> and trimming trees in a Chinese-style garden. It takes both time
> and efforts to grow a tree and to get it into a better shape.

In additional to 'planting' and 'growing' metaphors, there are environment metaphorical threads to Connie's ways of conceptualising the classroom. She talks on several occasions about trying to create a 'better climate for learning'.

Development or growth metaphors are also evident in her view of herself as a 'mother', as she begins to feel more comfortable in her teaching role. There is greater reporting of positive experiences 'now the students are willing to talk to me' and 'this class has become a family and I am the elder nurturing and scaffolding the youngers'. A close relationship of talk and advice is clear in this example:

> I guess I am like a mother but I don't always know what I am
> doing. At the beginning I was terrified of getting it wrong and
> there was a lot of advice. It made me think of my sister and her
> baby. There's always advice. It isn't easy to know which to follow.
> Some of it was in my head and other advice was in from my
> colleagues.

The consideration of which decisions to make seems to be linked to this idea of reflecting and acting on advice but knowledge, experience and 'advice' is sometime conflicting. However, as time goes on, Connie begins to take more account of 'what is working'. Like other students Connie reports 'pressure' from the 'dual-role as both an English teacher and 'as an administrative staff of the school' and there is a 'squeeze' between administrative work and commitment to English teaching.

Carmen

Carmen's root metaphor was an actress 'who tries to satisfy the audience as much as possible with her everyday performance'. She felt that the classroom is a space to 'involve the audience' and she referred to it 'a stage'. When we later revisited the metaphor she felt that the actress needed to be a magician and also a comedy act as well.

Interestingly in all the e-mails exchange with Carmen in her first year of teaching (and she was the most prolific) there are no instances of metaphor use in the area of acting, theatre, performance or stage. It may be that the reality turns out to be a little bit more mundane and humdrum than anticipated. However, she uses analogy and metaphor to a greater extent than the others. One theme that comes across strongly is her 'battle with time' connected to cooking metaphors. This is typical:

> I didn't get enough prep time and for the first few months I felt a
> little awkward because I had my busy timetable and it took me a
> while to get prepared for those lessons. You have the ingredients
> in the coursebook and some materials but not quite sure what
> quantities of this and amount of that. I like teaching and I consider
> myself a creative teacher, but I need much more time to get these
> recipes right.

Carmen sees her development as being like a cook and there's a feeling of trial and error and it is linked to awareness:

> Maybe at start of this year I was a junior cook. I have some half-
> remembered recipes but I think that experimenting by yourself
> and making it up is one of the best things to help you learn what
> works and what doesn't.

Cookery is certainly the most prominent metaphor and there are metaphors of 'mixing' and 'baking':

> When you're baking a cake you'll realize that ingredients, time, creativity and dedication all combined will make a good cake but it might not bake well the very first time. You may not get the mixture right. So you feel the experience and then you improve what you've done as long as you have your feet on the ground and watch the results.

A related metaphor, used in two different e-mails, concerns students' 'diet' and 'exercise' where 'each lesson is a special diet to improve the fitness or maybe the skills'. In these sessions there 'needs to be a variety of gym exercise and the right diet'. For Carmen 'the more you exercise and get the food right, the best shape and physical condition you can develop in the students'.

Like Connie there are occasional 'mother' metaphors. This choice may be influenced by her real-life care of her young son:

> Getting prep time is difficult for me since I have a son and a house to keep! It's been difficult for me to sort out my activities. I am always on the go and it's this work-life issue that is something I need to balance wisely.

Carmen uses the phrases 'maternal balance' and 'wise juggler' to capture her growing realisation that her role is about 'balancing sympathy, encouragement and support'.

Discussion

This study highlights reflective metaphor use in the first year of teaching. It provides examples of metaphor use in reflective writing. There are several key findings that are worth emphasis. First metaphor is used by first-year teachers to try and articulate particular difficulties, conflicts and tensions. Second, a large number of these metaphors are concerned with reaching some kind of balance and metaphors are often used to explain these 'balances'. In addition, there is little evidence that so called 'root-metaphors' are persistent.

Taken as a group, the case studies provide examples that support the view that teachers use metaphors as 'explanatory vehicles' (Block 1996: 51). The data suggests strongly that first year teachers feel pulled in different directions and are confused, faced by competing demands and choices. These demands and pressures come from students, colleagues, administrators, inspectors and parents. Metaphors are being used to articulate these concerns as teachers come to terms with these demands, while maintaining as much clarity as possible about the nature of the teaching experience (Bullough and Baughman 1997). The metaphors tend to be used in general comments (nature of things rather than specifics of particular teaching interventions). They tend to be attempts to encapsulate general feelings about the teaching experience and their general role, rather than at the level of the particular technique or procedure.

It is noticeable that a number of the metaphors are either about finding balance (in the physical sense of keeping standing up, 'one hand and another' or 'finding feet'). Clearly part of the challenge of the first year is to keep some sense of balance (Spencer 1986), to become more centred and connected (Palmer 1999), and to find 'somewhere to stand' (Clarke 2003). Difficulties are often constructed in exploratory metaphors of balance, footing and equilibrium. Farrell (2006b) provides a case study of a teacher as 'he balanced a delicate, and sometimes conflicting role'. In this case study Tom talks about 'developing a balanced teaching personae' that feels 'comfortable to him'. It seems to be important that these teachers are using metaphor to understand in order to then shape their response:

> If teachers are to be effective in adapting to and shaping the
> contexts in which they work, deliberate sense making of the real
> world conditions and day-to-day realities that influence teaching as
> well as personal ways of knowing about teaching, is vital. (Black
> 2001: 60)

The data offers evidence of metaphor helping to understand and potentially resolve dialogic tensions between:

- beliefs and reality

- administrative role and teaching role

- play and control

- teacher and student expectations

- seriousness and humour

- advice and experience

- CLT and discipline

- Outside expectations and individual choice

- Rewards and punishment

It has been recognised that first year teachers find it hard to get these kind of balances right and they consume a great deal of thinking time (Breeden and Egan (1997).

There is some evidence from this study that root metaphors persist (Massengil *et al.* 2005) in some form (Connie, Izumi and Tom). It is hardly convincing though and in two cases not detectable (Carmen and John). Really, only Connie shows evidence of much persistence. In fact, the evidence here suggests that the metaphors that teachers use change or at least that they use others for dialogic and exploratory purposes. I am not suggesting that the root-metaphors have necessarily changed. It seems much more likely that teachers simply 'try on' different metaphors. This study also suggests that metaphors become less optimistic in this first year.

Although studies of teachers' metaphors have recognised that core metaphors may be subject to change they have not sufficiently considered the possibility that they may be used essentially in temporary and dialogic ways, in other words as convenient ways of making sense. Metaphors are part of an ongoing dialogue between self-preservation and self-transformation (Kegan 1982: 45) and their adoption is probably more temporary and more dialogic than has previously been acknowledged. It may well be helpful to engage in teacher development activities that help to 'surface' teaching metaphors but there is also a danger in assuming that they are 'there' in some pre-existing way. If you ask teachers for a root-metaphor they might well provide one. However, it well be 'made up' in the here-and-now. Rather, such metaphor use may be convenient vehicles to explore current teaching tensions. Oxford *et al.* (1998) quoting Levi-Strauss (1966) say that analogical thought is not troubled by contradictions and there can be inconsistencies within expressed positions. Perhaps the point to make is more fundamental, in that metaphor functions to *explore* such contradictions and inconsistencies.

This study offers further support to the view that metaphors are central to the expression of issues of learner style and preference, methodological concepts and SLA constructs. Thornbury (1991) points out that metaphors such as 'language as matter' have been pervasive (language can be 'chunked' and 'segmented' and in fluid form 'filtered' and 'blocked'). For teachers metaphor becomes a short-hand for theory derived concepts ('monitor'(John); ' i+1' (Connie); ZPD (Tom); 'fossilising'

(Izumi)) and more practical metaphors ('jigsaw tasks' (Carmen); 'warmers' (Connie); 'top-down tasks' (Izumi)). For example, Carmen says:

> I think I'm getting more used to getting the level of difficulty right.
> I remember you talked about 'task tension' and I think I started off
> too ambitious with designing tasks. Then I tended to make them
> too easy. Now I'm getting a better sense of their ZPD.

This metaphor use shows a counterpoint to the view expressed by Zeichner and Tabachnick (1981) that first year teachers undergo a process of 'washing out' of the University course work. It seems that teachers are digesting MA programme input and continuing to try and describe mental acts and conscious processes by 'metaphorical means' (Elliot 1984: 38).

Conclusion

This chapter has presented as an exploratory case study of five language teachers teaching in different contexts but sharing the task of negotiating the tricky first year of language teaching. Perhaps the most striking finding is also the most obvious; there is a ubiquitous Catch 22 element to the first year of teaching. Just at the point where you need the most time for reflection is just the time when time is a particularly 'squeezed' commodity. The majority of the original group made clear that they do not have 'time' for any kind of reflective writing. Even the five who kept in touch found this difficult and it is clear that journal writing can quickly be seen as just another competing demand.

This study suggests that teachers do not hold on to so called 'core' or 'root' metaphors. There may be two possible reasons for this. The first is that their existence in any fixed way is open to doubt. The second is that they may be appealing in an educational context (University MA programme) but get supplanted with new metaphors used in exploratory ways. It is particularly striking that metaphors of balance are foregrounded in this sample, either in the actual metaphor or in close proximity to metaphor use.

Acknowledgements

I would like to thank the MA Education TEFL students at University of Birmingham for their honesty and willingness to share their experience of their first year of teaching. I would also like to thank Dr Fiona Copland at Aston University for her generosity in extensive comments on a draft of this chapter.

Note

1.   I have quoted teacher e-mails verbatim even when there are slight disfluencies. However, I do not intend to use 'sic' each time. However, the extracts have all been carefully checked.

References

Black, A. L. (2001). Grappling with the realities of teaching: Artful representations as sense making, meaning-making tools. In Singh, P. and McWilliam, E. Eds. *Designing Educational Research.* (pp 59–70). Flaxton: PostPressed.

Block, D. (1996). Metaphors we teach and learn by. *Prospect, 73.* 42–55.

Breeden, T. and Egan, E. (1997). *Positive Classroom Management.* Nashville, TN: Incentive Publications.

Bullough, R. V., Jr. (1991). Exploring personal teaching metaphors in preservice teacher education. *Journal of Teacher Education, 42* (1), 42–51.

Bullough, R. V. and Baughman, K. (1997). *'First Year Teacher' Eight Years Later: An Inquiry Into Teacher Development.* New York: Teachers College Press.

Bullough, R. V. and Knowles, J. G. (1991). Teaching and nurturing: changing conceptions of self as teacher in a case study of becoming a teacher. *Qualitative Studies in Education, 4,* 121–40.

Bullough, R. V. and Stokes, D. K. (1994). Analyzing personal teaching metaphors in preservice teacher education as a means for encouraging professional development. American. *Educational Research Journal,* 31(1), 197–224.

Burns, A. (1999). *Collaborative Action Research For English Language Learners.* Cambridge: Cambridge University Press.

Burns, A. (2005). Action research: an evolving paradigm? *Language Teaching 38* (2), 57–74.

Clark, C. M. and Peterson, P. L. (1986). Teachers' thought processes. In M. C. Wittrock (Ed.). *Handbook of Research on Teaching* (pp. 255–96). Macmillan: New York.

Clarke, M. A. (2003). *A Place To Stand: Essays For Educators In Troubled Times.* Ann Arbor, MI : University of Michigan Press.

Crandall J. (2000). Language Teacher Education. *Annual Review of Applied Linguistics 20,* 34–55.

Edge, J. (1992). *Co–operative Development: Professional Development Through Co–Operation With Colleagues.* Harlow: Longman.

Edge, J. (2002). *Continuing Cooperative Development*. Ann Arbor, MI: University of Michigan Press.

Elliot, R. K. (1984). Metaphor, imagination and conceptions of education. In W. Taylor (Ed.), *Metaphors of Education* (pp. 38–53). London: Heinemann Educational.

Farrell, T. S. C. (2001). Critical friendships: colleagues helping each other develop. *ELT Journal* 55: 368–74.

Farrell, T. S. C. (2006a). 'The teacher is an octopus': uncovering preservice English language teachers' prior beliefs through metaphor analysis. *RELC Journal* 37: 236–48.

Farrell, T. S. C. (2006b). Learning to teach English language: imposing order. *System*, 34 (2), 211–21.

Holliday A. (1994). *Appropriate Methodology and Social Context*. Cambridge: Cambridge University Press.

Johnson, K. E. and Golombek, P. R. (2003). 'Seeing' teaching learning. *TESOL Quarterly*. 37 (4), 729–37.

Kegan, R. (1982). *The Evolving Self: Problem and Process in Human Development*. Cambridge, MA: Harvard University Press.

Kelchtermans, G. (1999). Teaching career: between burnout and fading away? Reflections from a narrative -biographical perspective. In R. Vandenberghe, and M. Huberman (Eds) *Understanding and Preventing Teacher Burnout. A Sourcebook of International Research and Practice* (pp. 176–91). Cambridge: Cambridge University Press.

Kelchtermans, G. (1994). Biographical methods in the study of teachers' professional development. In I. Carlgren, G. Handal, and S. Vaage (Eds), *Teachers' Minds and Actions: Research on Teachers' Thinking and Practice* (pp. 93–108). London: Falmer.

Kenn M. (1996). Critical incidents in teaching and learning *Issues of Teaching and Learning* (28) http://www.csd.uwa.edu.au/newsletter/issue0896/critical.html (Accessed 22.03.06).

Lakoff, G. and Johnson, M. (1980). *Metaphors We Live By*. Chicago, IL: University of Chicago Press.

Levi-Strauss, C. (1966). *The Savage Mind*. Chicago, IL: University of Chicago Press.

Mann, S. (2003). Dialogic understanding. In M. Swanson and K. Hill (Eds) *JALT2003 Conference Proceedings* (pp. 246–55). Tokyo, Japan: The Japan Association for Language Teaching.

Mann, S. (2004). Evaluation. In Harnisch H. and Swanton P. (Eds) *Adults Learning Languages: A CILT Guide To Good Practice* (pp 113–29). London: CILT.

Mann, S. (2005). 'State-of-the-art: the language teacher's development'. *Language Teaching*. 38(3) 103–18.

Marti, J. and Huberman, M. (1993). Beginning teaching. In Huberman, M. *The Lives Of Teachers*. London: Cassell.

Massengill, D., Mahlios, M. and Barry, A. (2005). Metaphors and sense of teaching: how these constructs influence novice teachers. *Teaching Education.* 16 (3), 213–29.

Merriam, S. B. (1998). *Qualitative Research and Case Study Applications in Education* . San Francisco, CA: Jossey-Bass Publishers.

Munby, H. (1986). Metaphor in the thinking of teachers: an exploratory study. *Journal of Curriculum Studies.* 18 (2), 197–209.

Oxford, R., Tomlinson, S., Barcelos, A., Harrington, C., Lavine, R. Z., Saleh, A. and Longhini, A. (1998). Clashing metaphors about classroom teachers: Toward a systematic typology for the language teaching field. *System,* 26, 3–50.

Palmer, P. J. (1999). *The Courage To Teach: Exploring the Inner Landscape of a Teacher's Life.* San Francisco, CA: Jossey-Bass, Inc.

Prabhu, N. (1990). There is no best method – Why? *TESOL Quarterly* 24 (2), 161–76.

Roberts, J. (1998). *Language Teacher Education.* London: Arnold.

Schon, D. A. (1983). *The Reflective Practitioner.* New York: Basic Books.

Spencer, D. A. (1986). *Contemporary Women Teachers: Balancing School and Home.* New York: Longmans.

Stake, R. E. (2000). Case studies. In Denzin, N. K. and Lincoln, Y. S. (Eds) *Handbook of Qualitative Research 2nd edition* (pp 435–54). Thousand Oaks, CA: Sage.

Taylor, C. (1985). *Human Agency and Language.* Cambridge: Cambridge University Press.

Thornbury, S. (1991). Metaphors we work by: EFL and its metaphors. *ELT Journal,* 45 (3), 193–200.

Tobin, K. (1990). Changing metaphors and beliefs: A master switch for teaching? *Theory into Practice,* 29 (2), 122–7.

Wallace, M. (1991). *Training Foreign Language Teachers: A Reflective Approach.* Cambridge: Cambridge University Press.

Woodward, T. (1991). *Models and Metaphors in Language Teacher Training, Loop Input and Other Strategies.* Cambridge: Cambridge University Press.

Zeichner, K., Tabachnick, R., and Densmore, K. (1987). Individual, institutional, and cultural influences on the development of teachers' craft knowledge. In J. Calderhead (Ed.), *Exploring Teachers' Thinking* (pp. 21–59). London: Cassell.

Zeichner, K. M. and Tabachnick, B. R. (1981). Are the effects of university teacher education 'washed out' by school experience? *Journal of Teacher Education,* 22, (3), 7–11.

Zuzovsky, R. (1994). Conceptualizing teachers' knowledge about teaching: An advanced course in teacher education. *Studies in Educational Evaluation,* 20, 387–408.

3 Trained for teaching high school, poached for teacher training: a case study of a Cambodian teacher's first year of teaching in Cambodia

Stephen H. Moore

Introduction

This chapter is concerned with reconciling formal teacher training and actual classroom practice in the first year of a language teacher's career. A case study of the experience of a Cambodian English teacher's first year of teaching in Cambodia is presented. The teacher completed a four-year BEd (TEFL) degree to teach English in Cambodia's public secondary school system. By graduation, however, she had been recruited along with nine other graduates to replace a team of expatriate lecturers[1] and teach on the BEd (TEFL) programme itself. The chapter explores diverse issues as this teacher had to adjust to a demanding and high-profile teaching position for which she was not specifically trained. Among the issues discussed are: the adjustment from native-speaker expatriate lecturers to non-native-speaking local lecturers; the classroom management of unruly students; and gender relations in the language classroom. The research methodology (combining introspection, questionnaire and interview) provides a rich description of this teacher's personal account of her first and most formative year of teaching.

Background literature

As noted in Farrell (2006), little has been published about the first year experiences of language teachers, and this includes in the Cambodian setting. However, the Cambodian context in which this chapter is set has itself been well documented in Denham (1997) and Oats (1994). The central issue of transition from being an English language teacher to a TESOL teacher educator has been reported in Moore (2006) in terms of a Vietnamese context, but no similar research appears to have been published in relation to a Cambodian context. The important issue of native versus non-native speaker identities in the TESOL profession has been widely reported and discussed (e.g., Phillipson 1992; Pennycook 1994; Canagarajah 1999; Holliday 2005), but again nothing appears to have been published pertaining specifically to the Cambodian context. Classroom management issues have been researched (e.g., Wright 2005) but not specifically in relation to Cambodian classrooms. Lastly, gender in language classrooms has been widely researched in primary school classrooms, particularly in English-speaking countries (e.g., Julé 2005) and has been researched among Hong Kong teacher trainees (Forrester 1997) where it was found that the trainees themselves were reinforcing gender stereotypes in the classroom. There appear to be no published studies, however, of female university lecturers' experiences in terms of gender issues in Cambodian classrooms (however, see Fitzgerald *et al.* 1997, for an account of the experience of female students). Thus, the present chapter stands to contribute to many aspects of the gap in the language education literature pertaining to Cambodia.

Research methodology

Context

The destruction of Cambodia's education system during the Khmer Rouge regime (1975–8) is well known. It's reconstruction since 1979 has been a slow and arduous process (Ayres 2000) and remains a work-in-progress. Until 1988, the teaching of English in Cambodia was illegal. Following the Paris Peace Accords signed in 1991, Cambodia opened up to the outside world and English began to play an important role in the country's development. Given the scarcity of local teachers of English at that time, a concerted effort was made to increase the country's capacity to train English teachers. In this context, Sorida (a pseudonym) was admitted to the country's premier English language teacher training programme, the BEd (TEFL), at the Royal University of Phnom Penh.

The BEd (TEFL) programme was created in the early 1990s when a Quaker Service Australia aid project was converted into a teacher training degree programme known as the Phnom Penh University English and Education Project (PPUEEP), funded by AusAID and managed by a consortium of Australian educational institutions.[2] The degree programme was designed to produce high-quality English language teachers for Cambodia's high schools. The PPUEEP consisted of expatriate management and lecturers, whose numbers gradually reduced as they were replaced by Cambodian counterparts. The project officially ended with the departure of the last AusAID-funded expatriate manager, but the BEd (TEFL) degree programme continues to thrive up to the present time.

The four-year degree consisted of three years of intensive English language instruction (i.e., 'Core English', Literature Studies and Cultural Studies) followed by a fourth year of teacher training (e.g., Foundations in Education, Applied Linguistics, Teaching Methodology and Teaching Practicum). The programme began with a small number of students, but enrolments steadily increased in the early years as shown in Sorida's workplace was the Institute of Foreign Languages, custombuilt in the 1960s and refurbished in the early 1990s. The academic year ran from late September to late June, and was divided into two semesters. In Sorida's first year of teaching, teachers received a fixed salary of US$250 per month,[3] paid by AusAID. Most lecturers were given teaching duties in two or more subject areas and would focus on teaching one or two levels. They typically had between 20 and 30 hours of weekly contact teaching with their students. Each subject area for each year had a lecturer acting as coordinator (e.g., Literature studies Year 1 coordinator), who was responsible for ensuring standards were set and met. Teachers of a particular subject and year would collaborate to create appropriate end-of-semester tests. A Director of Studies was responsible for the overall management of the BEd (TEFL) degree programme.

Table 3.1: BEd (TEFL) student enrolments in early years

Year	*1993/4*	*1994/5*	*1995/6*
1	96	100	100
2	38	96	100
3	45	38	96
4	48	45	38
Total	**227**	**279**	**334**

Source: Adapted from Phnom Penh University English and Education Project Graduation Ceremony Program, 29 June 1995.

Prior to commencing her duties as a lecturer on the BEd (TEFL) programme, Sorida had very limited teaching experience consisting of three short episodes. First, she taught an evening English class to approximately 50 ethnic Cham students for four months. Then she taught English for beginners to approximately 20 interested learners from her neighbourhood. Lastly, as part of her Year 4 studies, she participated in the High School teaching practicum where she taught a class of approximately 65 students over a six-week period.

Sorida's teaching load in her first year of teaching after graduating consisted of approximately 20 contact hours per week, split between Core English (at two levels) and Literature Studies (at one level). Class sizes for Year 3 were typically 25 students, while the Year 1 classes were slightly larger. The Core English classes met three times per week, while the Literature Studies classes met twice per week. Each lesson was 90 minutes in duration. Sorida's rough teaching load is set out in Table 3.2.

In addition to teaching, lecturers were responsible for formulating ongoing assessments (worth 40 per cent of the final grade) and contributing to the development of end-of-semester summary tests (worth 60 per cent). Ongoing assessments consisted of a mix of several written assignments, short tests and oral assessments.

Methodology

The research reported in this chapter uses a case study methodology, exemplifying an interpretive research paradigm. As such, it makes no claims to be generalisable to the experience of other Cambodian teachers faced with similar circumstances to Sorida's, nor indeed to any other similar circumstances that might be found outside Cambodia. Its value as research lies in its close attention to important details as seen through

Table 3.2: Sorida's teaching hours during her first year of teaching

Subject	New	Repeat	Total
Core English Yr 1	4.5	—	4.5
Core English Yr 3	4.5	4.5	9.0
Literature Studies Yr 3	3.0	3.0	6.0
Total	12.0	7.5	19.5

the eyes of the case study subject herself, but prompted through the purposeful nature of the researcher's questions.

After receiving clearance from Macquarie University's Ethics Committee to conduct this research with Sorida,[4] the author collected relevant data as follows. First, Sorida was given two statements (Appendix 3.1) and asked to introspect about them and to write some brief notes for the researcher over the subsequent 36 hours. After collecting these notes, the researcher administered a four-page questionnaire (Appendix 3.2) on which Sorida again wrote her responses. The following day, after having viewed the questionnaire responses, and in light of the introspection notes, the researcher interviewed Sorida using a semi-structured interview format (Appendix 3.3). The interview was transcribed by the researcher over the following two days. The complete data, constituting a rich description, were then further analysed and interpreted for the purpose of writing an account of Sorida's first year of teaching.

Findings

This section will introduce Sorida's main responses to various prompts from the data collection instruments. These are then elaborated in the subsequent discussion section.

Preparedness and support

Sorida agreed that she had been well-prepared to teach in Cambodian secondary schools, and cited evidence from her six-week practicum placement in which she did well and had enjoyed the experience. Sorida also agreed that she had been (unintentionally) well-prepared to teach in the BEd (TEFL) degree programme itself since having graduated from it she was familiar with the appropriate teaching techniques as well as the content.

When asked at what stage she had felt confident that she was doing her job well, Sorida indicated this was the case as early as the end of the first week of teaching. However she added a note of caution to any sense of overconfidence: 'There were always ups and downs … throughout the year. Sometimes I finished my day with joyous feelings, but sometimes I had a grim feeling that something could have been done differently [and perhaps better].'

When asked who had provided the most important support to her do enable her to do her job well in her first year of teaching, she nominated her fellow teachers (who, through being former classmates, were also friends).

Key issues as determined by Sorida

Sorida identified six issues which were, at the time, the key issues for her in her first year of teaching. She grouped them into two sets: institutional and personal.

The institutional issues that presented significant challenges were concerned with: (1) the programme's transition from being taught by native English speakers to being taught by Cambodians; and (2) the programme's introduction of a student 'contribution' fee where previously students had paid nothing towards the cost of teaching materials and handouts.

The four personal issues that Sorida identified as being significant during her first year of teaching were: (1) the pride and responsibility associated with being a university lecturer; (2) the issue of teaching classes in which as many as half the students had not done their homework; (3) the preparation necessary to deal with trouble-makers; and (4) the resistance of some students to the communicative teaching methodology used.

Discussion

In terms of Sorida's preparedness for her first year of teaching, she presents a persuasive case that she was well prepared to teach English as a foreign language whether in high schools or in a university teacher education programme setting. Her experience of high school teaching in her practicum provided valuable feedback that she could handle the challenges of that kind of teaching, at least on a week-by-week basis. She was wise enough to concede that frustrations might mount if she were to teach in high schools on a month-by-month or year-by-year basis. In that case, she would have had to adapt to the reality she faced, including the constraints of limited teaching resources and large class sizes. In terms of her actual teaching at university level, Sorida drew on her experience as a university student. She could refer both to her own notes as a student (since she had studied the same content as she was required to teach), but also to the experience of how the expatriate teacher taught the particular subject. In other words, she could model her teaching on that of her own expatriate teachers.

The ability (and an awareness of that ability) to deal with diverse teaching situations equipped Sorida with a strong sense of self-worth and confidence which were important elements of her teacher persona. As previously mentioned, she was one of ten new lecturers, all recent graduates, recruited at the same time. They joined the existing team of seven Cambodian lecturers to comprise the first full cohort of exclusively Cambodian lecturers teaching the BEd (TEFL) programme. Sorida nominated the support of her fellow first-year teachers and their camaraderie as the most important form of support contributing to her doing her job well in her first year of teaching. Such support was vital in sustaining Sorida's self-belief and self-confidence then, as she was able to deal with the 'ups' and 'downs' that were (and are) an integral part of the rhythm of university-level teaching.

Turning to the institutional issues that Sorida identified as being particularly significant in her first year of teaching, during her final year of studies half of her teachers were expatriates and half were Cambodian lecturers. When she began teaching as a lecturer, her students were faced with the reality of having no more expatriate native-speaking lecturers. It fell to the individual lecturers to deal with student concerns about this policy change. Sorida immediately felt the students' 'resistance, resentment and distrust' directed at her as a non-expatriate lecturer. She confronted them directly about the issue, admitting that her English was not perfect but her role was to facilitate student learning, and that she would do her very best to help them learn in her lectures. Over time the student body adjusted to the new reality and got on with learning. By the end of the academic year, most students were resigned to the fact that they would not be taught by expatriates. It was clear by then that the new system had not only survived, but had been placed on a very sound footing through the hard work of a talented group of young Cambodian lecturers.

Although the issue of 'Cambodianising' the BEd (TEFL) programme had been flagged many months in advance of its inception, another institutional issue arose that had not been foreseen either by the lecturers or the students. This concerned the introduction of a student contribution fee of US$80 per year towards the costs of teaching materials. The student contribution fee was an initiative of the expatriate programme manager, who oversaw the discretionary AusAID funding for the BEd (TEFL). The contribution fee was a significant amount of money in

Cambodia, and the students were deeply unhappy about it. Many students, perhaps most, refused to pay it. Even the lecturers were unhappy about the fee's impact. It meant that the number of photocopies for handouts used in daily teaching had to be drastically cut back in order to match the level of student contribution funding. Although this did not affect Sorida's own teaching to a significant degree (i.e., her Core English classes followed the Headway coursebook series while the Literature Studies classes followed novels of which each student had a private copy), the students' unrest and agitation did unsettle the new lecturers at a sensitive time in the early weeks of their first year of teaching. The matter was finally diffused within a few weeks when the programme manager backed down and eased the restrictions on photocopies, but the contribution fee was strongly promoted and, within a few years, was no longer contested.

Turning to the four personal issues mentioned by Sorida as being particularly significant in her first year of teaching, the pride in being selected as a lecturer on the BEd (TEFL) programme was a source of great satisfaction and confidence for Sorida. At the same time, however, she realised that she had a responsibility to be able to live up to the high expectations placed upon her by PPUEEP and the university authorities. At the risk of losing face, for example, she always carried a pocket dictionary when teaching, and was not afraid to refer to it if necessary when teaching. This might have surprised her students and exposed her to a higher degree of scrutiny by them, but she found that her students had to accept that it was in their best interests that she look something up rather than hazard a guess that might be wrong and then go uncorrected.

Another significant issue for Sorida in her first year of teaching was having to deal with students who did not do their homework. This was a particularly vexing issue in respect of teaching Literature Studies where a number of assigned pages from a novel were meant to be read in anticipation of the follow-up lecture. As many as half the students might come to class unprepared, not having done their homework. This was a new experience for Sorida and she dealt with it through her own ingenuity. When scolding proved to be an ineffective strategy, she would sometimes collect homework and mark it as part of the ongoing assessment grade. Another technique she employed was to have students work in groups where she would ensure that at least one member of every group had in fact done the homework and therefore was able to assist the others. She also had a longer term strategy that aimed to stimulate and garner the latent interest students might have in literature as they became more aware of 'hidden' meanings and the power of literary works. They might then become more interested in exploring the subject and more aware of how the assigned homework could facilitate their interest.

Dealing with troublemakers was another significant issue that Sorida had to face early in her first year of teaching. She adopted what could be described as a 'no-nonsense' approach. Rather than ignore a troublemaker, she would confront him[5] directly. Her strategy was to give the troublemaker the floor to express his opinion for an extended period of time (e.g., five or ten minutes). Then, she would reclaim the floor and demand that the troublemaker listen attentively to what she had to say, as she had done in listening to him. This strategy also had the benefit of giving her the 'last word' in discussing the issue. What is most interesting to note here is how the majority of students would then rally to defend Sorida's position and thus ostracise the troublemaker from his peers. It was largely peer pressure on the troublemaker that diffused the situation, leaving Sorida's reputation enhanced and her 'control' of the class consolidated.

The fourth issue that Sorida identified as significant was the student resistance she sometimes faced towards her teaching methodology. As previously mentioned, she modelled her teaching on that of the expatriate lecturers who had taught her the same content. It is curious that many Cambodian students found the same teaching methodology to be acceptable for an expatriate lecturer but not for a Cambodian lecturer. Obviously this was a source of frustration for Sorida. She cited an interesting example involving the interpretation of a passage in a novel being studied in Literature Studies. She would present multiple interpretations and the evidence for each, and leave it to the students to decide which they felt was best. Some students, however, would persist in asking her which interpretation was 'actually right'. Sorida herself had no trouble accepting the fact that there was no one 'right' answer, but it was a challenge for her to convince many of her students that they too could and should view literary works in that light. She continually made the point that a reasoned argument was always needed, that is, one in which evidence from the text is used to support claims made in an interpretation. So long as this advice was followed, she promised to retain an open mind about how well students 'understood' texts.

The last issue to discuss here is one that was prompted by the researcher, rather than raised by Sorida herself. It concerns the issue of gender in the language classroom and, in particular, the case of a female teacher in a predominantly male environment. (In fact, of the 17

Cambodian lecturers on the BEd (TEFL) programme, only three were female, including the non-teaching Director of Studies). The PUUEEP wanted to recruit as many competent female lecturers as possible but, given the scarcity of female role models in positions of authority in Cambodia, it was unclear whether this policy would work both for the lecturers and the students. In response to the questionnaire, Sorida indicated that she disagreed that being a female teacher with mostly male colleagues made her job more difficult. On the contrary, she pointed out that it was well known that the Cambodian lecturers were selected on the basis of academic merit and their teaching ability. The fact that she had finished at the top of her graduating class put her, she felt, in a strong position among her colleagues. She was respected for what she knew, and was not resented as being a 'token' female. 'Our work was judged by its quality, not [according to] gender differences.'

Likewise, Sorida disagreed that being a female teacher with predominantly male students made her job more difficult. 'In fact, I felt that my gender worked in my favour. I could use my charm as a smart female teacher to win their hearts.' As for the few male students who would not take her seriously, she noted that they had little choice but to follow her rules and instructions in the classroom. Regarding the issue of being a role model for female students, Sorida expressed the view that she did not see herself in that light, but accepted it was possible that female students might see her that way. 'I treated my students as equal individuals. I didn't do special things for female students.'

Conclusion

This account of a Cambodian English teacher's first year of teaching has offered an insider's view of a personal history set within a well-defined background of both institutional and political change. The experience she gained in her first year of teaching set the stage for Sorida's subsequent successful English language teacher training in Cambodia. Her teaching knowledge and skills were not, however, developed in a vacuum. She was a top graduate herself, full of enthusiasm for teaching and a strong determination to succeed. Her solid English language skills complemented her shrewd ability to analyse various teaching situations and to develop appropriate solutions to problems that arose. The combination of these factors enabled Sorida to win over an initially sceptical community of language learners – disappointed not to be taught by native English speakers – and to help them learn.

References

Ayres, D. M. (2000). Tradition, modernity and the development of education in Cambodia. *Comparative Education Review, 44* (4), 440–63.

Canagarajah, S. (1999). *Resisting Linguistic Imperialism*. Oxford: Oxford University Press.

Denham, P. A. (Ed.). (1997). *Higher Education in Cambodia: Perspectives of an Australian Aid Project*. Canberra: University of Canberra.

Farrell, T. S. C. (2006). The first year of language teaching: Imposing order. *System, 34*, 211–21.

Fitzgerald, L., Bounchan, S. and Pauv, A. (1997). Planning for gender equity in the language classroom. In P. A. Denham (Ed.), *Higher Education in Cambodia: Perpsectives of an Australian Aid Project* (pp. 69-81). Canberra: University of Canberra.

Forrester, V. (1997). The challenge of gender-bias reform: A case study of teacher trainees in Hong Kong. *Asian Journal of English Language Teaching, 7*, 113–19.

Julé, A. (2005). Gender and linguistic space in a language classroom. *Multilingua, 24* (1/2), 25–37.

Holliday, A. (2005). *The Struggle to Teach English as an International Language*. Oxford: Oxford University Press.

Moore, S. H. (2006). From chalkboard to lectern to chalkboard: the journey of an applied linguistics lecturer. In T. S. C. Farrell (Ed.). *Language Teacher Research in Asia* (pp. 107–22). Alexandria, VA: TESOL.

Oats, W. N. (1994). *I Could Cry for these People*. Hobart, Tasmania: Quaker Service Australia.

Pennycook, A. (1994). *The Cultural Politics of English as an International Language*. London: Longman.

Phillipson, R. (1992). *Linguistic Imperialism*. Oxford: Oxford University Press.

Wright, T. (2005. *Classroom Management in Language Education*. Basingstoke: Palgrave Macmillan.

Appendix 3.1: Introspection questions

1. Do you remember what were, **at the time**, the key issues for you in your first year of teaching?

2. **Reflecting back now** (with ten years of language teaching experience), what were the key issues for you concerning your first year of teaching?

Appendix 3.2: Survey questions

- I think I my BEd (TEFL) degree program prepared me well to teach in Cambodian secondary schools.

  [Strongly agree, agree, no opinion, disagree, strongly disagree]
  The main reason for this view is: ___________________________

- I think I my BEd (TEFL) degree program prepared me well to teach in the BEd (TEFL) program itself.

  [Strongly agree, agree, no opinion, disagree, strongly disagree]
  The main reason for this view is: ___________________________

- Being a female teacher with predominantly male colleagues made my job more difficult.

  [Strongly agree, agree, no opinion, disagree, strongly disagree]
  The main reason for this view is: ___________________________

- Being a female teacher with predominantly male students made my job more difficult.

  [Strongly agree, agree, no opinion, disagree, strongly disagree]
  The main reason for this view is: ___________________________

- I saw myself as a role model for female students.

  [Agree, no opinion, disagree]
  Why or why not? ___________________________

- I was trained to teach English in Cambodian secondary schools. My job at the Institute of Foreign Languages required me to teach three or four different subjects every week. This aspect of my first year of teaching was difficult.

[Strongly agree, agree, no opinion, disagree, strongly disagree]

- Teaching 'Core English' was easy.

[Strongly agree, agree, no opinion, disagree, strongly disagree]
The main reason for this view is: ________________________________

- Teaching '(English) Literature Studies' was easy.

[Strongly agree, agree, no opinion, disagree, strongly disagree]
The main reason for this view is: ________________________________

- Teaching 'Foundations in Education' was easy.

[Strongly agree, agree, no opinion, disagree, strongly disagree]
The main reason for this view is: ________________________________

- Supervising the teaching practicum was easy.

[Strongly agree, agree, no opinion, disagree, strongly disagree]
The main reason for this view is: ________________________________

- I felt confident that I was doing my job well by

    □ the end of the first week
    □ the end of the first month
    □ the end of the first semester
    □ the end of the first year
    □ other (please specify):________________________

- The most important support for me to do my job well in my first year of teaching was from my:

    □ family
    □ friends
    □ fellow teachers
    □ centre's administrators
    □ students
    □ other (please specify):________________________

END OF SURVEY

Appendix 3.3: Interview questions

1. Please describe any teaching experience you had prior to graduating with your BEd (TEFL) degree.

2. Please describe your first semester's workload (e.g., number of classes; number of students in each class; typical lesson duration; number of lessons per week; number of repeat lessons per week; assessments per semester; number of assignments marked each semester etc.)

3. In Cambodian culture older teachers are typically respected for their experience. As an inexperienced teacher not much older than your students, (i) how did your youthfulness impact on your classes? (ii) How did you deal with this issue?

4. Many students at the Institute of Foreign Languages were unhappy that the native English speaking teachers were being replaced by non-native English speakers. How did you handle this situation? Can you recall any specific incidents with any particular students?

5. Is there anything else you would like to tell me about your first year of teaching that you haven't mentioned?

Notes

1. The author was one such expatriate lecturer.
2. The consortium consisted of IDP Education Australia; the University of Canberra; and the National Centre for English Language Teaching and Training at Macquarie University.
3. Per capita income at the time was approximately US$20 per month, so these teachers were well-paid.
4. Disclosure was made to the Ethics Committee that Sorida was a family relation of the author's through marriage.
5. Troublemakers were invariably male.

4 Learning to teach language in the first year: a Singapore case study

Thomas S. C. Farrell

Introduction

Novice teachers must deal with many pressures during their first year of teaching because learning to teach in that first year, as Doyle (1977) has suggested, not only involves 'learning the texture of the classroom' but also learning how to deal with different 'sets of behaviors congruent with the environmental demands of that setting' (p. 31). Thus novice teachers must not only learn how to deal with important structural influences that can occur (mainly at the classroom level), but they must also learn how to balance more personal influences that can arise from other individuals the teacher interacts with during the first year, especially other colleagues (Farrell, 2003). This chapter outlines how a first year language teacher attempted to balance a delicate, and sometimes conflicting, role between learning to teach and learning to become a teacher within an established school culture in a neighbourhood secondary school in Singapore.

Background literature

Learning to teach is a complex process because the learning does not only take place during the first year alone; other influences have an impact on how the first year teachers are socialised into the profession such as the influence of their previous schooling, the influence of the teacher education programme itself, and the influence of the first year socialisation process. While it is beyond the scope of this chapter to detail all these influences, the influence and impact of previous schooling is very strong on what novice teachers do during their first year because of the long hours while they were students watching their teachers and developing images (usually tacitly held) about teaching and learning. Another influence on novice teachers during their first year is the formal teacher education programme they have graduated from but its real impact on what novice teachers implement from it in their actual teaching many in fact be limited (Richards and Pennington 1998). Richards and Pennington (1998) for example, discovered in their study of Hong Kong novice language teachers that the context and the realism of the classroom had a more influential role in deciding on what the novice teachers implemented in their teaching rather than try material they had learned in the teacher education programme.

However, recent research has indicated that one of the most influential factors in determining the success or failure of teacher socialisation during the first year of teaching is the nature and type of relationships the novice teachers form (or fail to form) with their colleagues (Williams *et al.* 2001). For instance, research has indicated that it may be the case that several different 'teacher cultures' may exist in one school (Carew and Lightfoot 1979) and colleagues can be considered either as guides and guardians (Zeichner and Tabachnick 1985) where they take an active role in helping the novice teacher adapt to the new school, or a more passive role as a 'confirming source of influence' (Jordell 1987: 171). Williams *et al.* (2001) have further noted that if a first year teacher's colleagues do not help a novice teacher adapt to their new surrounding and pursue a culture of individualism (as opposed to collaboration) within that school, it will result in 'at worst, potentially damaging to the NQT [newly qualified teacher] development and at best, damaging to the longer term interests of the school' (pp. 256–7). Consequently, support and cooperation from their experienced colleagues, and usually in the form of a mentor, may be crucial because novice teachers have found their first year a period of great anxiety (Johnson 1996).

That said, mentoring relationships, defined as taking place when 'a knowledgeable person aids a less knowledgeable person' (Eisenman and Thornton 1999: 81), may be unpredictable because some mentors may feel unclear about their roles and responsibilities that may have been pushed on them just because of the years of experience they have accumulated as teachers. However, as Tomlinson (1995) has noted, as experienced teachers 'they may have become so intuitive they find it difficult to articulate what in fact they are doing' (p. 18). Nevertheless, research has indicated that novice teachers who are mentored tend to be more effective teachers in their early years since they learn from guided practice rather than depending upon trial-and-error efforts alone. Thus mentors need to have a clear set of roles that they understand and can articulate to the novice teacher. Within English language teaching, Malderez and Bodoczky (1999: 4) describe five different roles that mentors can play: (1) they can be models who inspire and demonstrate; (2) they can be acculturators who show mentees the ropes; (3) they can be sponsors who introduce the mentees to the 'right people'; (4) they can be supporters who are there to act as sounding boards purposes, should mentees need to let off steam; and (5) they can be educators who act as sounding boards for the articulation of ideas to help new teachers achieve professional learning objectives. Malderez and Bodoczky (1999: 4) suggest that most mentors will be involved 'to a greater or lesser degree in all five roles'. What follows is an account of the challenges one novice English language teacher in Singapore encountered as he negotiated his first year in the profession.

Research methodology

This study utilised an interpretative approach (e.g., Lacey 1977) to Wee Jin's (a pseudonym) socialization and development as a teacher during his first year. Such an approach seeks to understand a teacher's development from the perspective of the individual teacher (rather than the observer) and attempts to show the influence of the unique elements of each individual teacher's passage through his/her first years. For this we focused on his specific context, the school, and how he interpreted his own process of becoming a teacher during his first year (Zeichner and Tabachnick 1985; Kuzmic 1993). Consequently, qualitative (Bogdan and Biklen 1982) rather than quantitative methodologies were used.

Data were collected from the following sources: the researcher's field notes and written-up log, six hours of classroom observations, transcriptions of classroom data and post-observation conferences, semi-structured interviews with the teacher and the school principal (transcribed and coded), and regular journal writing on the part of the beginning teacher. The data were initially analysed using a procedure of data reduction, and confirmation of findings. During data analysis, the interviews were transcribed for accurate interpretation of emergent patterns and themes. The interviews, discussions, journal entries and classroom observations were coded by inductive analysis procedures (Johnson 1992). As data were analysed on a continuing basis throughout Wee Jin's first year of teaching, instances of the phenomenon under study were labelled; labels, or concepts, were compared one against another and those sharing the same characteristics were entered under a category. In order to impose some order and clarity, categories were further developed into a story structure framework for first year teachers (Farrell, 2006). This story structure follows a pattern of *orientation – complication – result* and is explained as follows. The *orientation* part of the narrative addresses questions such as: Who is involved? When did it take place? What took place? Where did it take place? The *complication* outlines the problem that occurred along with any turning points in the story. The *result* part discusses how the complications were handled by the teacher and were they resolved. Thus the story structure framework was superimposed on the narrative and descriptive data as 'a way of getting a handle on what we believe, on models, metaphors and images that underpin action and enable meaning making, on our theories' (Bullough 1997: 19).

Setting

Singapore, the setting of this case study, has a heterogeneous multi-ethnic population of more than three million people. Singapore has four official languages: English, Mandarin, Malay, and Tamil; other languages and dialects also abound on the island. It is not easy to classify the position of the English language in Singapore because there are Singaporeans who use English as a first, second or foreign language (Gupta 1998); however, English has been the medium of instruction in the school system since 1987 (Xu and Tan 1997). Regarding the teaching of the English language in the schools in Singapore, Foley (1998) has observed that recently methodologies have been moving slowly from teaching English as a foreign language to 'methodologies of English as the dominant language of education – using a first-language approach to teaching' (p. 248). He points out that the model of English in the classroom will often show that it has been adapted into so-called 'Singlish' (Singapore Colloquial English).

Wee Jin enrolled at the National Institute of Education (NIE), Singapore for a one-year programme, the Post Graduate Diploma in Education (PGDE), to certify him as a secondary school teacher in Singapore. He came to the NIE with a BA (English language and Mathematics) degree (all PGDE students enter with a degree). The students in the PGDE program take a ten-month program in which they are exposed to teaching practice and theory classes. After successfully completing this course, Wee Jin was posted to a neighbourhood secondary to teach English language. According to Wee Jin, the students at the school were 'mainly from the middle to lower middle classes' (Wee Jin's journal). At the time of the study I was an English language teacher educator at the National Institute of Education (NIE), Singapore. I first met Wee Jin when he was my student during his PGDE course. I asked him if I could explore his development during his first year as a teacher by talking with him frequently and observing some of his classes, and he agreed to this.

Findings

Complications

Wee Jin faced a number of complications during his first year as a teacher, and because of space limitations, I can only discuss three of these. Wee Jin's first complication concerned conflict between his approach to teaching English language and what was expected from the school and the head of the English department. His second complication was conflict between what he wanted to teach (the content), and what he was required to teach. His third major complication concerned the difficulties he had with various professional relationships (other teachers and the administration) in school during his first year. Wee Jin's own words are used whenever possible to describe each of these.

Complication 1: teaching approach

The first complication concerned a conflict between how Wee Jin was expected to teach in contrast to how he had wanted to teach, and this was focused mainly on his desire to take a learner-centred approach to instruction which he defined as 'lots of student-to-student interaction in the form of pair work and group work during class because this type of interaction in an English language class leads to effective learning of the language' (pre-classroom observation I discussion). However, when he began to teach actual classes, he said that he realised it would not be easy to adopt this strategy because he had noticed a different tradition of teaching in the school that was firmly teacher-centred in approach. Wee Jin remarked: 'although many teachers at the school paid lip service to learner-centred teaching, I saw many teacher-centred classes' (pre-observation I discussion). He also mentioned that this teacher-centred approach was in conflict with what he had learned in the teaching education courses, and that his new colleagues commented that it would not work in 'the real classroom because it creates high noise levels in classrooms and this has negative consequences for controlling students' (pre-classroom observation I discussion). In fact, he said that some teachers suggested that they considered a class where students are sitting in groups and talking loudly 'an example of bad teaching, or at the very least, inadequate classroom management skills on behalf of the teacher' (pre-classroom observation I discussion). Wee Jin suggested that, 'The teachers' main fear is that the use of groups would lead to a loss of control on teachers' part' (Wee Jin's journal). Wee Jin also noted that the culture of the school 'frowned upon a high volume of noise that they associated with increased student-to-student interaction' (post-study interview). So, it seems, then, that early in his first year he had to find ways of dealing with this dilemma: how to reconcile the differences between his belief that a student-centred teaching approach can lead to more effective learning than the more established traditional teacher-centred approach that existed in that school. As Wee Jin noted, 'I don't know how to make my lessons more pupil-centred without infringing school regulations such as noise level, pupil movement and control of the class' (Wee Jin's journal).

Complication II: course content

Another major complication Wee Jin faced during his first year was conflict between what he wanted to teach in terms of course content, and what the department, and especially the department head, required him to teach. For example, when planning his English language lessons, Wee Jin said that he was faced with the dilemma of how to balance what he believed his students needed in educational content and the department's established syllabus. Wee Jin said that this syllabus required him to use 'certain department-produced materials in the English lessons' (Wee Jin's journal), and that this in turn limited the extent to which he could try out new teaching ideas in class. Wee Jin continued: 'Other requirements give me a limited opportunity and time for trying out new teaching ideas in class because I have to use materials for composition and comprehension lessons' (Wee Jin's journal). This predicament led to a further complication of how to adequately prepare his students for the rigorous examination system in the school if he did not follow the department's syllabus exactly. Wee Jin, noted that this school exam system influenced the preparation of his lessons because he realised that it 'has to have a great influence on the content I will teach' (Wee Jin's journal). As such, he realized that if he 'included too many course materials regardless of their educational value that were not going to be tested on the examination, then my students might be at a disadvantage' (Wee Jin's journal). Nevertheless, Wee Jin said that he believed his students 'needed to be educated rather than just prepared for tests and that is why I want to bring in outside materials from different sources' (pre-classroom observation II discussion).

Complication III: collegial relationships

A third major complication that Wee Jin faced concerned the degree to which he formed professional relationships with colleagues and administrators during his first year. Wee Jin said that he realised early in the year that he found himself posted in a school that 'exhibited a culture of individualism' (Wee Jin's journal). He said that he was basically left on his own throughout the year. Wee Jin remarked that he 'didn't talk much with the other teachers because they were always busy and into cliques ... only two new teachers [from the same teacher training institution] are here' (post-study interview). Wee Jin said he observed different types of teachers at his school as follows:

> I see three types of teachers [in the school]: the group that came
> together three years before [from the teacher training institution] ...
> I think there are seven of them. The older teachers transferred
> from other schools all stick together. Also, we have the old
> teachers who have been here a long time and keep to them-
> selves. (Post-study interview)

Related to professional relationships, Wee Jin said that as the year progressed he was experiencing greater difficulty understanding the general culture of the school, and the English Department, 'in terms of the decisions that were made, especially in the English department' (post-classroom observation II discussion).

Result

Throughout his first year Wee Jin said that he attempted to resolve the various complications he experienced, and as outlined below, he had mixed success.

Teaching approach

As stated previously, Wee Jin experienced conflict between his belief about the efficacy of a learner-centred teaching approach and a teacher-centred approach that was already firmly in practice and even expected, in the school. Wee Jin said that throughout his first year as he attempted to reconcile these differences, he did not want to give up his belief in the importance of including student interaction in his classes 'whenever I can' (pre-classroom observation III discussion). He noted that at the end of his first year his teaching approach was 'to a certain extent, also shaped by my pupils' perceptions of how a 'good' English lesson should be conducted' (post-study interview). Wee Jin also noted that he felt his whole approach to teaching was constrained throughout his first year because he could 'not follow a teacher-centred approach regardless of what was expected by the school' (post-study interview). At the end of his first year, this tension remained, to a certain extent, unresolved.

Course content

Wee Jin said that regardless of the content the department head (HOD) required him to teach, he decided he would remain 'more responsive to his students' needs' (Wee Jin's journal). To this end, Wee Jin said that throughout the second semester of his first year, he continued to 'bring in extra materials' from his 'own resources to augment the textbooks' (post-study interview). He said that he told his students not to be worried about these extra materials because they would also 'cover what the department required' (post-study interview). Wee Jin said he had to reassure them about these materials because he noted that his students seemed concerned about their relevance to examinations they would be faced with. So he said that he continuously reassured them that they would be 'prepared for whatever skills the department syllabus advocated' (post-study interview). For example, he said he was adamant that his students learn reading strategies because the required textbooks were 'only concerned with testing reading, not teaching it' (Wee Jin's journal). So Wee Jin said that he prepared sets of materials that would help his students practise reading strategies and other such skills not covered in the textbooks. Nevertheless, Wee Jin also said that he was very much aware of the examinations his students would sit at the end of the year and that he realised the significance of these examination results for his students' futures. He remarked: 'If common tests are all focused on reading comprehension, I will tend to equip my pupils with comprehension-related skills. This is how I survived as a student' (post-study interview).

Collegial relationships

Of the three complications Wee Jin was faced with during his first year as a teacher, collegial relationships proved to be the most difficult for him to resolve, if he ever did. I am not sure if the reason for this unresolved dilemma is because of the culture of individualism that existed in the school, or because of Wee Jin's reluctance to ask for assistance throughout his first year, or a combination of both. For example, even though Wee Jin was assigned a mentor teacher from the school to help him through his first year as required by the Ministry of Education in Singapore, he noted that this mentor only met with him on his first day in the school; and as Wee Jin noted, 'I never had any further contact, professional or otherwise, with this teacher again' (post-study interview). Additionally, Wee Jin said that he did not at any point during his first year teaching strike up a relationship with any other member of staff, 'either a mentor, or any other experienced teacher I could go to for advice' (post-study interview). This is problematic because research has indicated that support for teachers in their first year may be crucial for their survival through this period (Johnson 1996). This support, especially in the skills of teaching and of the emotional kind, should come from the school authorities and from colleagues within the school (Odell and Ferraro 1992). It is interesting to note that in a discussion about Wee Jin's progress during his first year, the school principal noted that he had complied with all the school rules and seemed to be 'progressing nicely' (school principal interview). When I mentioned this to Wee Jin later, he said that although he gave the impression that he was complying with the school rules and policies, he also retained his private reservations and doubts about what he was required to do.

Discussion

Wee Jin seems to have gone through several stages during his first year as a teacher. First, he entered the school with some early idealism characterised by a strong identification with the students, as he really wanted to make a difference in their lives. He also rejected older cynical teachers at the school. He then suffered some shock from the reality of the classroom as he moved through his first semester as a teacher. In his quest to survive this phase, Wee Jin sought quick fixes for the discipline problems he was experiencing with one of his classes, but he still encountered some difficulties with the class and his communication with his colleagues. He next entered a phase of beginning to recognise these difficulties and their causes, but he also wondered if he would make it as a teacher. He wrote about this when he was bewildered with all the reading and marking of the exam scripts: 'I thought I was the "misfit" in the department' (Wee Jin's journal). These reflections began towards the end of the first semester and the beginning of the second semester.

As the first year progressed, Wee Jin began to cope better with his classes (his teaching methods and classroom management). He had established certain routines for himself both inside and outside the classroom and was trying to fit into the culture of the school. Maynard and Furlong (1995) call this phase 'reaching a plateau'. Wee Jin had also started to enter Maynard and Furlong's (1995) final phase called the 'moving on' phase as he was beginning to pay more attention to the quality of his pupils' learning. However, I cannot say that he followed each phase in a sequential manner and he may have been experiencing more than one phase at any one time, while lapsing back into a previous phase. I would say that he was continually moving back and forth between Maynard and Furlong's (1995) final three phases: recognising difficulties, reaching a plateau, and moving on. Towards the end of the first year Wee Jin began to focus on the quality of his student's learning as he began to realise that his real reason for being a teacher was to meet his students' needs: 'I think that all students always come first. If a particular programme of course of action will benefit them, I will endeavour to carry it out. If it's not going to benefit the students, I will scrap it or play it down' (Wee Jin's journal).

The main purpose of presenting Wee Jin's story of his first year as a language teacher is not necessarily to highlight the actual complications he was faced with and the various resolutions he attempted (although these are very important). The main aim is to highlight that language teachers in their first year of teaching will invariably be faced with an array of complications that can hamper their development if they are not resolved, or if not, at the very least, they should come up with some understanding of what these complications are, if they are to continue teaching. However, language teacher education programmes have a history of emphasising 'How to teach' with its main stress on methods rather than what it means to be a language teacher. Consequently, I suggest that language teacher education programmes move away from stressing the various methods of teaching language and move towards promoting development of skills in anticipatory reflection so that beginning teachers become more aware of what they will face when they make the transition from the teacher education programme to the real world of the classroom. As the results of this Singapore case study indicate, development of this type of reflection is especially important if new teachers want to try out practices they learned in teacher education programmes or seek to deviate from the traditional practices and expectations that are firmly in place in the new setting. Activities that can encourage anticipatory reflection in language teacher education programmes include analysing written up case studies that follow a story structure framework such as the one reported in this chapter. As Jalongo and Isenberg (1995) pointed out, this type of story framework can offer preservice teachers 'a safe and nonjudgmental support system for sharing the emotional stresses and isolating experiences of the classroom' (p. 162). Anticipatory reflection can be further enhanced by linking the case study analysis to classroom observations, journal writing and class discussions that are part of many teaching practice assignments. In this way preservice language teachers cannot only reflect on their teaching methods, but also reflect on the socio-historical contexts in which they find themselves placed for the practicum. Research in general education has indicated that the professional culture of each school can present many challenges for first-year teachers and thus has an enormous influence on their development and as such, these novice teachers require support from teacher education programmes and the schools in which they are placed (Kardos *et al.* 2001; Williams *et al.* 2001). Wee Jin realised this at the end of his first year when he said that: 'New teachers need a lot of affirmation and support to pull through the first year. Obtaining feedback without worrying about any negative implications would also go a long way in helping teachers to grow' (post-study interview).

In addition, and in order to build up a corpus of the experiences of first year language teachers that use the story structure framework to impose order, further case studies should be carried out by either replicating the methodology (a qualitative study approach) outlined in this chapter, or by establishing a different research design. Regardless of the methodology used, it is very important that the 'researched' teacher has the opportunity to read and respond to the researcher's portrayals and interpretations of their work – as I have done in the case study reported earlier. If there are any disagreements between the researchers and the researched, then these can be negotiated and greater insight can be achieved by all involved. Better still, mutual constructions of the 'story' by the researcher and the researched should be encouraged. In this way, studies about first year teachers can be considered research for the teachers rather than research on the teachers. These stories and their results can be fed back into the language teacher education programme curriculum so that language teacher educators can think more carefully about the consequences of the content of the curriculum they have in place and if this curriculum is really preparing teachers for their first year as a teacher.

Conclusion

This chapter presented a case study of how a first year language teacher balanced a delicate, and sometimes conflicting, role between learning to teach and learning to become a teacher within an established school culture in a neighbourhood secondary school in Singapore. The chapter also suggests that the use of a 'story structure' framework (*orientation – complication – result*) may be one method of imposing some order on the various descriptions of first-year teaching experiences so that language teacher educators can overcome the perception that all first year teaching experiences are so unique that we cannot impose some order on the array of different experiences they encounter in their classrooms so that beginning teachers can be better prepared to make a smooth transition from their teacher education programmes into the real world of the language classroom.

References

Bogdan, R. and Biklen, S. K. (1982). *Qualitative Research for Education: an Introduction to Theory and Methods*. Boston, MA: Allyn and Bacon Inc.

Bullough, R. V. (1997). Becoming a teacher: self and the social location of teacher education. In B. J. Biddle, T. L. Good, and I. F. Goodson (Eds) *International Handbook of Teachers and Teaching* (pp. 79–134). Boston, MA: Kluwer Academic Publishers.

Carew, J., and Lightfoot, S. L. (1979). *Beyond Bias: Perspectives on Classrooms*. Cambridge, MA: Harvard University Press.

Doyle, W. (1977). Learning the classroom environment: An ecological analysis. *Journal of Teacher Education*, 28, 51–5.

Eisenman, G. and Thornton, H. (1999). Telementoring: Helping new teachers through the first year. *T.H.E. Journal*, 26 (9), 79–82.

Farrell, T. S. C. (2003). Learning to teach English language during the first year: personal influences and challenges. *Teaching and Teacher Education*, 19, 95–111.

Farrell, T. S. C. (2006). The first year of teaching: Imposing order. *System*, 34 (2), 211–21.

Foley, J. A. (1998). Language in the school. In J. Foley, T. Kandiah, Z. Bao, A. F. Gupta, L. Alsagoff, C. Ho, L. L. Wee, I. S. Talib and W. Bokhorst-Heng *English in New Cultural Contexts: Reflections from Singapore* (pp. 244–69). Singapore: Oxford University Press.

Gupta, A. F. (1998). The situation of English in Singapore, In J. Foley, T. Kandiah, Z. Bao, A. F. Gupta, L. Alsagoff, C. Ho, L. L. Wee, I. S, Talib and W. Bokhorst-Heng *English in New Cultural Contexts: Reflections from Singapore* (pp. 106–26). Singapore: Oxford University Press.

Jalongo, M. R. and Isenberg, J. P. (1995). *Teacher's Stories: From Personal Narrative to Professional Insight*. San Francisco, CA: Jossey-Bass.

Johnson, K. E (1992). Learning to teach: instructional actions and decisions of preservice ESL teachers. *TESOL Quarterly*, 26 (3), 507–35.

Johnson, K. E. (1996). The vision versus the reality: The tensions of the TESOL practicum. In D. Freeman and J. Richards (Eds), *Teacher Learning in Language Teaching* (pp. 30–49). New York: Cambridge University Press.

Jordell, K. O. (1987). Structural and personal influences in the socialization of beginning teachers. *Teaching and Teacher Education*, 3, 165–76.

Kardos, S., Johnson, S., Peske, H., Kauffman D. and Liu E. (2001). Counting on colleagues: New teachers encounter the professional cultures of their schools. *Educational Administration Quarterly*, 37, 250–90.

Kuzmic, J. (1993). A beginning teacher's search for meaning: Teacher socialization, organizational literacy, and empowerment. *Teaching and Teacher Education*, 10, 15–27.

Lacey, C. (1977). *The Socialization of Teachers*. London: Methuen.

Malderez, A and Bodoczky, C. (1999). *Mentor Courses: A Resource Book for Teacher-Trainers*. Cambridge: Cambridge University Press.

Maynard, T. and Furlong, J. (1995). Learning to teach and models of mentoring, In T. Kelly and A. Mayes (Eds). *Issues in Mentoring* (pp. 10–20). London: Routledge.

Odell, S. J. and Ferraro, D. P. (1992).Teacher mentoring and teacher retention. *Journal of Teacher Education 43*, 200–4.

Richards, J. C. and Pennington, M. (1998). The first year of teaching. In J. C. Richards (Ed.) *Beyond Training* (pp. 173–90). New York: Cambridge University Press.

Tomlinson, P. (1995). *Understanding Mentoring: Reflective Strategies for School-based Teacher Preparation*. Buckingham: Open University Press.

Williams, A. Prestage, S, Bedward, J. (2001). Individualism to collaboration: The significance of teacher culture to the induction of newly qualified teachers. *Journal of Education for Teaching 27* (3), 253–67.

Xu, D, and Tan, P. L. (1997). Trends of English use among Chinese Singaporeans. In A. Brown (Ed.) *English in Southeast Asia 96, Proceedings*, pp. 54–66. Singapore: ELAL, NIE.

Zeichner, K. M. and Tabachnick, B. R. (1985). The development of teacher perspectives: social strategies and institutional control in the socialization of beginning teachers. *Journal of Education for Teaching*, 10, 1–25.

5 Occupational socialization in the first year of teaching: perspectives from Thailand

David Hayes

Introduction

It has long been recognised that the process of learning to become a teacher is complex and may be fraught with tensions and anxieties for novice teachers (Bullough *et al.* 1991; Rogers and Babinski 2002; Ryan 1970). These tensions and anxieties are not confined solely to the realities and immediate demands of coping with students in classrooms, issues of maintaining discipline, enacting methods, using materials, and engaging with students to attempt to influence learning; but also extend to establishing the teacher's place within the institutional context of the school, encompassing such factors as relating to colleagues, learning the norms of behaviour expected in the school, and often managing one's identity as a teacher within the local community served by the school. Kelchtermans and Ballet (2002: 106) contend that 'this organisational socialisation constitutes an essential task for teachers as much as their classroom teaching'. In order to comprehend fully beginning teachers' experiences, enquiry needs to go beyond classroom teaching to encompass what happens as novice teachers become members of organisations with their own cultural-ideological and concomitant social-professional interests (Kelchtermans and Ballet 2002; Farrell 2003). Every school has a culture of norms, values and ideals to which teachers are expected to subscribe and every school is a complex web of interpersonal relationships which may engender a series of different teacher cultures within the school (Farrell 2003). Fitting into a school as a member of an organisation is, then, a process which can be fraught with pitfalls for the novice teacher just as much as coping with classroom realities. In this chapter I describe how a group of Thai teachers of English working within their state educational system dealt with the complexities of being a teacher and what this meant for them in their institutions primarily as members of school organisations with subsidiary reference to their roles as classroom teachers. Links are made to the experiences of beginning teachers in other contexts portrayed in the general educational literature and a plea is made for a stronger research focus in TESOL on the multifaceted nature of induction for beginning teachers of English in order to inform teacher education programmes.

Background literature

Though pre-service training is supposedly designed to prepare students for life as a teacher, often novice teachers find themselves ill-equipped to cope with the transition from the role of student in a teacher-training institution to qualified teacher in a school, particularly in relation to aspects of organisational socialisation. The notion of the first year of teaching as a 'reality shock' or 'praxis shock' is commonplace. As Rogers and Babinski (2002: 1) put it: 'False expectations, shattered dreams, and serious attacks on one's competence and self-worth – these are the all too common experiences of beginning teachers.' 'Praxis shock' is a widely observed phenomenon across the world, noted, for example, by Kelchtermans and Ballet (2002) in Belgium, Tafa (2004) in Botswana, So and Watkins (2005) in Hong Kong and Flores and Day (2006) in Portugal.

A number of researchers have placed the experiences of beginning teachers within frameworks of career development. Sikes (1985), for instance, in a study of 48 secondary school teachers in the United Kingdom, uncovered what she saw as a common developmental sequence in teachers' careers, from entry into the profession until retirement, irrespective of the idiosyncracies of individual biographies. These were banded by age-group into 'phases', beginning with those from 21–28 years of age. Sikes found that these early years have a provisional, exploratory quality with careers not being fixed. Teachers are evolving their personal pedagogies and often face 'critical incidents' concerning maintenance of discipline, a crucial area of concern for the beginning teacher as challenges to authority are seen as challenges to professional identity. They are also subject to the pressures of socialisation into occupational cultures which may be inimical to their own personal philosophies: stories of disillusionment amongst young, idealistic teachers are legion. Similarly, Huberman (1993), in his study of 160 teachers in Switzerland, characterises the first phase as a period of 'survival and discovery'. In this phase beginning teachers are concerned with 'five fundamental aspects of the profession: relationships with students; mastery of the knowledge base or subject taught; relationships with colleagues; relationships with the institution (status, function); and lastly, the teachers' perceived preparedness for the profession' (Huberman 1993: 195–6). In characterising the phase as a period of survival *and* discovery, Huberman brings balance to the received wisdom of the first year of teaching solely as 'reality shock'. Clearly there is substantial evidence to show that for many beginning teachers their first year is indeed just such a reality shock, as there is all too often a 'distance between ideals and the daily realities of the classroom' (Huberman, 1993: 244), but Huberman also notes that for the teachers in his study this was counterbalanced by the theme of discovery which 'has to do with the enthusiasm of beginning a career with experimentation, with the pride that comes from having one's own students, one's own programme and, finally, with feeling part of a professional guild' (Huberman 1993: 244). This reminds us that the experience of beginning to teach is not necessarily a negative one and that – as we ought to expect – 'a degree of variability exists in the relative success of beginning teachers' (Hebert and Worthy 2001: 899).

Though there are numerous studies which explore the experience of beginning teachers in general education, there is little comparable research in the TESOL literature despite the avowed importance attached to this phase for future career development (Richards and Pennington 1998). An exception is Farrell's (2006) case study of the process of professional socialisation of a Singaporean high school teacher of English. Farrell (2006: 219) suggests that there is a need for replication studies to 'build up a corpus of the experiences of first year language teachers' and in what follows is an attempt to contribute to this corpus.

Research methodology

Participants' contexts

The contexts in which the teachers in this study had their early teaching experiences were government secondary schools in north-east Thailand. Thai education is regarded as 'traditional' (here used to indicate an approach unsuited to the contemporary world and, indeed, to the goals of the current school curriculum) and authoritarian in nature (Chayanuvat 2003). Although English is not a compulsory subject in the Thai curriculum, virtually all schools teach the language. Teachers in Thailand are traditionally expected to impart knowledge to their students and most classes are teacher-fronted and controlled. The predominant teaching style is expository. Even where textbooks are supposedly communicative in orientation, teachers will often read out dialogues and other texts, ask the students to repeat them and then translate the dialogue or text into Thai. No value judgement is made as to whether the communicative approach in whatever manifestation is desirable but it should be pointed out that the learner-centred methods which are integral to the approach are also legislated for in the most recent National Education Act for all subjects (Office of the National Education Commission 1999: 35). In harmony with official pronouncements, schools use textbooks which purport to be 'communicative' and stress student involvement in learning, but, as suggested, the books may be taught in other ways and teaching styles remain predominantly transmissive.

Initial teacher-training for one of the participants in this study was at a local Teachers' College and for the remaining three it was conducted at a university in the north-east of the country which was renowned for its English language teacher education. However, teachers' perceptions of this renowned institution were rather different. One of the participants, Aruneee, lamented:

> The instructors in university don't know what the real classroom in
> secondary level are [like]. They teach what they have learnt, what
> they are trained in western country, in Europe, in America, but
> they don't know the real classroom.

(Criticism of the lack of practical relevance of initial teacher-training courses is, of course, not confined to Thailand and dates back at least as far as Lortie's (1975) seminal work *Schooteacher.*) After graduation, those who wish to join the ranks of the government teaching cadre are required to pass a 'Teacher's Examination'. For English teachers this is focused not just on their subject – English – but also encompasses psychology, educational measurement and evaluation and bureaucratic knowledge of the 'teacher's law'. Curiously, it seems that universities and colleges do not prepare their students for this examination but graduates have to study by themselves, in spite of the fact that the kind of knowledge required for the teachers' examination is central to what teachers need to know as professionals in government schools.

Data collection

The research data for this chapter arises from a series of in-depth, unstructured interviews with four Thai teachers of English, each interview lasting between 2–3½ hours. The unstructured interview aims to 'provide access to the meanings people attribute to their experiences and social worlds' (Miller and Glassner 1997: 100) and the conduct of such interviews is of paramount importance. There is ample guidance on conducting in-depth interviews in the literature (Chirban 1996; Kvale 1996; Gillham 2000; Wengraf 2001; Rubin and Rubin 2005) and all writers agree that a central characteristic of this type of interviewing is that it 'becomes more like a conversation between partners than between a researcher and a subject' (Schutt 1999: 304). Achieving this conversationality when there is inevitably a power imbalance in most interview situations, the undertones of researcher and researched roles resonating throughout the process, is a skilled process which requires practice. Interviews for this study were not conducted at the first time of meeting; and two of the four participants cited in this chapter were, in fact, known to the researcher in a professional capacity for some time prior to the interviews. I did not wish the interviews to be constrained by a schedule and preferred to let the conversation evolve once a topic had been broached in very general terms as, for example, with the question 'How did you become a teacher?' I had, then, to rely on my skill as a listener/interviewer and 'think on my feet' in order to facilitate the progress of the interview. This did not mean, though, that I was controlling the interview in anything other than a very general sense. In these interviews there was little danger of the question-answer dyad typical of a structured interview acting as a control technique. What participants had to contribute thus arose directly from their own recollections of the experience of their first year of teaching, unconstrained by overt interviewer direction.

Participants

The four female Thai teachers whose interviews have been drawn on for this study were in mid-career and thus reflecting on their experiences in the first year of teaching, which had happened some time previously. That they were able to recall them so vividly is a testament to their enduring power. All of the teachers began their teaching careers in government secondary schools in the north-east of Thailand and they have been anonymised as Arunee, Naraporn, Sasikarn and Sudarat.

Findings

Once Thai teachers have passed the formal 'Teacher's Examination' it seems to be assumed that they are ready to play a full part in the life of a school as soon as they are appointed. As Arunee commented:

> They just come, say you are a teacher, you get appointed and
> then you have to find your own way.

None of the Thai teachers in this study experienced any formal process of induction beyond an initial meeting with the institution head, being introduced to fellow teachers by the head of department and to the student population during a school assembly. Another teacher, Sasikarn, noted that the onus was very much on the incoming teacher to find out what she or he needed to know. (In the quotations 'I' refers to the interviewer.)

> You find somebody, the school won't do anything for you. You
> have to find somebody, probably the first person that I met or the
> first person that I have to share the house, the teachers' housing
> with. Or the teacher, one teacher in the department that will teach
> with you ... with me, like co-teacher ...
>
> I: Co-teaching the same course, not the same class?
>
> Yeah same course, not same class. (Sasikarn)

This 'sink or swim' approach does not just apply to school administrative systems and procedures but also extends to the level of the curriculum which the teacher is supposed to implement. Sasikarn went on to describe the process of being told about her teaching duties thus:

> [I was told] Here's your room Ajarn, this is English Department,
> that's your table and this year you're going to teach E101 for M1
> [Secondary 1], for example ... And then you have to take another
> course as well for M2, and then another course for M3, are you OK
> with that? What should I say? I have to say OK. [Laughs] You don't
> even have time to look at, you know like make decision whether
> you would like to teach that course or not but you have to accept
> it. That's first thing. Second thing they will say, this is another
> coursebook we have for you. This is from last year. Oh this is the
> pile of books: you can choose by yourself which one you are

> going to teach and then we will order that for students. [...] Yes,
> after that have to, you know, look at the coursebook and then start
> planning the lessons. (Sasikarn)

Being given the textbook as the sole guide to the curriculum was widespread, as is confirmed by Arunee's experience.

> I don't know what the curriculum was when I was the teacher at
> first. I don't know. I didn't see the curriculum, no-one gave it to
> me. When I start my career in the school, the head of the depart-
> ment gave me the book before I went to class. I don't know what
> the curriculum was and I don't care. I follow the book and I think
> the book is the curriculum

Similarly, Arunee had to find her own mentor from whom to learn about the regulations and the routines of the school but, rather than searching out a sympathetic colleague as Sasikarn suggested, she was able to look within her family for this guidance, supplementing it by a 'look and learn' approach.

> My husband teach me. He gave me suggestions because he is
> from the family that his father and mother are teachers but for me
> my father and mother are merchants [...] and I observe by myself,
> learn, keep learning by doing. Sometimes I did something wrong
> and I learn later I should not have said that, I should not have done
> that, learn by myself.

These teachers' views make clear the emphasis placed on the personal responsibility of the teacher during socialisation into the life of the school. Teachers have to – and most do – learn from experience in the 'sink or swim' approach. Arunee went on to contrast her initial experience with her knowledge two years later when she moved to her present school.

> But when I came here [present school] I am a more learned
> person. I know how to speak, how to behave. Because when I
> freshly graduate from university I speak what I think, but now
> sometimes I speak what I don't think. [Laughs] You have to learn.
> [...] I don't agree with some things but for peace I have to be silent.

Here she emphasises that learning to be a teacher is not just a matter of knowing what to do in the classroom but is as much a matter of knowing how to operate in the school culture – entailing on occasion saying things which one does not believe in order to maintain group harmony. This is an aspect of school life which, as her own experience testifies, beginning teachers are ill-equipped to deal with. She herself learnt in her first year that it did not always do to say what she thought but that at times it was better to say what she didn't really believe. This is not something which features in any teacher education curriculum in Thailand.

Though there is little doubt that the informal methods described by Arunee and Sasikarn are able to assist new teachers in adapting themselves to the realities of the professional culture, Arunee herself expressed a wish for initial teacher training courses to better prepare teachers for life in schools, to develop courses with a focus on 'practical things, how to call the roll, how to keep records' rather than just concentrating on subject content, methods and psychology. However, it is interesting to note that when asked about processes of induction in her present school now that she was in a position of authority as head of department, she had not taken the opportunity to remedy the deficiencies of the initial training courses in universities which she had identified.

> I: Is there anything that you do with your new teachers when they
> come to the school to help them learn about the department or
> the school; or anything the school does?
>
> Er no, I don't do that because they are supposed to be trained
> from the university . and when they come into the school it's their
> workplace, they should be confident already so I don't think I will
> have to train them.

Instead she relied on the informal mentoring system that seemed to be common practice in most Thai schools – 'I will ask someone who teach in the same level to supervise them' – illustrating, perhaps, the power of institutional custom in this respect. Certainly, it indicates that with regard to induction nothing seems to have changed since Arunee and the other teachers in this study began to teach.

For another teacher, Naraporn, coming to terms as a new teacher with the life of the school seemed to be more of a social process than even an administrative one. Reflecting on how her department welcomed her as a teacher and how similar processes have continued since, she emphasised the close knit nature of teachers in her department as a social group with concerns extending into personal lives: 'We live like family as I told you. [...] I like the way we help even, you know, serious problems, even personal things we can talk.' For her, initiation into school routines, ways of teaching and administrative procedures seemed to come a distant second to the social.

> We are, you know, all of us are very nice and then we welcome
> them [new teachers], make them feel like home, you know. We
> didn't let her or him alone by himself. When we go out and then
> we have party, we have picnic and then welcome them. Not only
> welcome as formal 'I would like to welcome you' no, but we made
> it, you know, informal and very easy to get familiar.

Processes of induction for new teachers can thus achieve the important goal of acquiring social solidarity with one's colleagues. Once social solidarity is achieved beginning teachers may then be at liberty to pursue their own professional paths.

The data thus illustrates that the process of occupational socialisation can take a variety of forms. It can be accomplished in formal ways such as the introductions at school staff meetings and school assemblies which most informants recorded. It can also be achieved informally in very powerful and important ways on a social level through the incorporation into a social group which Naraporn especially valued. These are positive experiences. However, there are other, less constructive, informal ways in which socialisation into the particular occupational culture of an institution can be achieved – or at least attempted. Sudarat's initial experience as a beginning teacher in the school where she herself had been a student illustrates negative aspects of informal socialisation. In her first year of teaching she attempted to use a communicative approach in her own classes, having herself experienced and enjoyed this as a student. However, her new colleagues – some of them her own former teachers – reacted in an extremely negative way. She found her authority constantly challenged and undermined by the actions of some more senior teachers.

> I had my students do some group work or pair work, you know,
> and they made a loud noise so I was scolded by the older teachers,
> you know, even though I'm a teacher. I stand in the front of the
> class and they complain me. [...] I don't want to teach in the first
> year because I couldn't do anything because I'm the ex-student
> here. It means I'm always a student and not the teacher. [...]
> Because most of the teachers want the students to be very quiet. I
> don't like that way.

Had she not herself been a student in this school it is much less likely that her colleagues would have treated her like this. However, being respectful towards one's teachers is a very strong cultural tradition in Thailand, persisting even beyond the period of formal education, and so Sudarat could not directly confront this behaviour. Instead she not only had to maintain harmony in her workplace by trying to keep as low a profile as possible but also had to encourage her own students to keep their feelings in check. In the interview she returned to the difficulties of her first year time and time again.

> The first year I want to retire. I told my mother I don't want to teach here, I don't want to be a teacher, because I can't do anything that I want to. Every time when I teach [senior teachers said] 'Sudarat's class again' …
>
> I: Because they were noisy?
>
> Yes [they] scold my students when I stood in the front of the class. I went to the bathroom and I cry and I cry a lot, and my students you know they will – demonstrate?
>
> I: Yes, protest.
>
> Yes, protest, yes but I told them not to do that because they I think they felt pity … but I say 'No, please don't, please don't do anything'. Because they're good students you know … They like the way I taught them and they thought that English is easy when they study with me and they can enjoy studying. … When I make a loud noise, when my students make a loud noise, when I come back to my staffroom I have to walk quietly – I don't like that way.

It is significant here that Sudarat recalls the affection of her students which, it seemed, was a primary source of support and enabled her to continue teaching even though in her first year she often felt she wanted to quit the profession.

It is not necessarily universal, of course, for students who become teachers in their own schools to perceive being treated as a student negatively. Even in this restricted data set there is counter-evidence that a new teacher can manage the situation so that she maintains her professional integrity. Naraporn, who also returned to teach in her old school, perhaps made greater allowances for her own teachers' tendency not to realise she had grown and that her role had changed. As she said:

> I can work with them very well […] I can adjust myself quite well. […] Sometimes they said 'Come and help me dear. Can you help me?' like before [when she was a student]. Yes, I can do it but, you know, things easy for me here; nothing, not a problem for me here in working.

Experiences of socialisation in the first year of teaching are inevitably diverse within an education system, and even where specific circumstances seem to be similar responses to those circumstances may well be different. Nevertheless, the data illustrate that there are also commonalities in the experiences of teacher socialisation in Thailand, even though one must acknowledge the restricted nature of the data set and so the grounds for any generalisability. What participants in this study tell us may be regarded as illuminative of the situation, a contribution to the corpus of experiences of first year language teachers which Farrell (2006) calls for.

Discussion

Whatever the diversity of these teachers' experiences the key issue remains the importance of the experience of beginning to teach on a teacher's subsequent career. A number of themes for discussion arise from the data. .

Self-socialisation

Thai schools according to our informants are isolationist with regard to professional practice. Perhaps one of the determining influences on the continuation of this culture of professional isolation is the socialisation into such cultures that beginning teachers experience: they are 'trained for isolation' (de Lima, 2003) in their early years of teaching and have to sink or swim in their first year. Lack of a formal programme of induction is not uncommon in other educational contexts. In the Netherlands, beginning teachers have similarly felt 'that they were left to their own resources' and that 'the initiative to build good relations with colleagues should come from their side' as Brouwer and Korthagen (2005: 202) discovered. In Botswana too Tafa (2004: 757) discovered that: 'On joining the teaching profession new teachers easily succumb or fit into to the highly authoritarian school socialisation processes, not least because they are thrown in at the deep end in a "sink or swim" fashion with no formal programme of induction.' Self-socialisation as a feature of induction into teaching is not new and not restricted to Thailand: it has been noted since Lortie's (1975) study more than 30 years ago and continues until today in many countries on different continents as we have seen. However, though many teachers do learn to adapt to the exigencies of a new school and adapt to its culture, it is highly questionable whether this is the most effective way to help novice teachers begin their professional careers. The experience of participants in this study would indicate that more thorough preparation for all the roles that a teacher has to fulfil in school, as well as some guidance in dealing with the formal structures of schools as organisations and with one's teacher colleagues would alleviate some of the heavy demands that are placed upon teachers in their first year in school.

Mentoring

Learning institutional norms of behaviour is patently more difficult for beginning teachers within a culture of professional isolation than within a culture of collaboration. In common with many other contexts (see e.g. de Lima 2003) Thai schools have developed systems in which year group teachers are supposed to co-ordinate their work but these tend to be more formulaic than to provide any genuine opportunity for collaborative endeavour. There is no system for mentoring of new teachers even though the importance for novice teachers of 'a properly trained mentor ... [acting] as a bridge between the new and the more established teachers at the school' (Farrell 2003: 104) has been documented. It could be argued that in finding somebody from whom to learn about school life, whether within the school in the case of Sasikarn or from outside in the case of Arunee, new teachers cope with this lack of formal mentoring by searching out their own informal mentors. But, although these informal mentors assist with learning the administrative requirements of a school and provide information about social groupings, there is no evidence in the data for this study that the mentoring process extended to matters of classroom practice which is equally important to new teachers. As participants noted, when Thai teachers begin teaching they are usually informed of their classes, given books they are expected to use and tend to see the textbook as curriculum, whatever their previous training. Again, this is similar to current experience elsewhere. In Brouwer and Korthagen's study of 357 Dutch beginning teachers of various subjects it was noted that 'teaching was influenced to a large degree by the textbook currently prescribed in their schools' (Brouwer and Korthagen 2005: 203).

Socialisation by established teachers

But, even though classroom mentoring of beginning teachers is rare, visions of acceptable pedagogy may still be determined by senior colleagues in an institution in an informal way – as Sudarat discovered. It seems to be common for established members of a teaching community to attempt to socialise newcomers into ways of working that may be contrary to their own beliefs and teachers in their first year may find it very difficult to resist these pressures. As Nias (1985: 117) puts it, new teachers 'sometimes align their frames of reference more closely with those of their colleagues' in order to fit in with a prevailing school, or school sub-group, culture. But the peculiarity of the situation in which new teachers returning to the place of their own schooling continue to be treated as if they were students does not seem to have been recorded beyond Thailand. Sudarat was not the only teacher in this study to begin her teaching in the school where she was a student. Another teacher, Ladda, whose experiences have not been focused on in this chapter, suffered a similar experience when moving back to her own secondary school and complained in almost the same terms.

> It's like I'm – always they [other teachers] think you are a student.
> It's one thing they think.

The method that Sudarat found to cope with the situation – affirming her value as a teacher through the responses of her students – is not an uncommon reaction to teachers experiencing non-teaching difficulties in schools. Research elsewhere has shown that teachers tend to look towards their students as a 'reference group' (Nias 1985) and derive their primary source of professional satisfaction from them, a satisfaction which can enable them to continue to teach when other conditions are not conducive.

Socialisation and TESOL

As yet there is little engagement in TESOL with the broader aspects of induction discussed by participants in this research. Exceptions are Farrell's case studies dealing with teacher induction into the institutional life of a particular school, one in a general educational journal (2003) and one in a TESOL journal (2006). The experience of socialisation of an English teacher in Singapore echoes that of the Thai informants in this study with respect to the lack of support in coming to terms with the complexity of a teacher's life, even though in Singapore mentoring by experienced colleagues was officially mandated for beginning teachers. To cope with the lack of support Farrell suggested that responsibility for induction was not the sole responsibility of the school but that the teacher him or herself needed to 'become more proactive' in defining his/her needs as a beginning teacher prior to taking up a post (Farrell 2003: 107). Other research also shows that effective teachers are active participants in their own development even in the first year of teaching (Hebert and Worthy 2001). In this respect, the participant in this study who seemed to have most difficulty within her institution, Sudarat, stood her ground and continued to teach in the way that she believed most effective, despite the attempts of her colleagues to influence her to change her practice.

Another aspect of teacher socialisation uncovered in this study of Thai teachers, the social processes of induction as illustrated by Naraporn were not mentioned in Farrell's (2003) study, however, (nor in Johnson 1996; or Richards and Pennington 1998) and do not seem to feature elsewhere. Neither is the peculiar position of individuals returning as teachers to schools in which they had once been students, and finding themselves still treated as students, replicated elsewhere in the TESOL literature. These provide clear indications of directions for further research.

Conclusion

Processes of teacher induction and the socialisation of beginning teachers have received some attention in the TESOL literature. Yet, as with other areas of research in TESOL, this has been primarily focused on the classroom and concerns the ways in which pedagogy learnt on a pre-service teacher education course is mediated – even abandoned – following contact with the realities of teaching (see, e.g., Johnson 1996; Richards and Pennington 1998). At the root of these modifications or abandonments of practices taught in pre-service education was the cognitive dissonance experienced by the teachers between their visions of teaching and the realities that they faced, leading Johnson (1996: 47) to conclude that there was a 'need for [language] teacher preparation programmes to put forth a realistic view of teaching that recognizes the realities of classroom life'. Whilst accepting the value of exploring 'a realistic view of teaching' in TESOL teacher education programmes, research in this study would seem to suggest that it is not just 'the realities of classroom life' that need to be explicated but the realities of schooling as a whole, including processes of induction into school and departmental life, as teachers' working lives consist of so much more than classroom teaching. There would seem, then, to be a case for a much stronger research focus on the multifaceted nature of induction for beginning teachers of English in their first year of teaching in order to uncover experiences which could then be used, as both Johnson (1996) and Farrell (2003) suggest, to inform teacher education programmes so that they might then offer beginning teachers the knowledge and skills necessary to deal with all aspects of their lives as teachers, not just the pedagogic.

References

Brouwer, N. and Korthagen, F. (2005). Can teacher education make a difference? *American Educational Research Journal*, 42 (1), 153–224.

Bullough, R. V., Knowles, J. G. and Crow, N. A. (1991). *Emerging as a Teacher*. London and New York: Routledge.

Chayanuvat, A. (2003). English learning experiences of Thai students enrolled at a university: a case study. In Hull, J., Harris, J. and Darasawang, P. (Eds) *Research in ELT. Proceedings of the International Conference 9–11 April 2003*. Thonburi, Thailand: School of Liberal Arts, King Mongkut's University of Technology Thonburi.

Chirban, J. (1996). *Interviewing in Depth: The Interactive-relational Approach*. Thousand Oaks, CA: Sage Publications Inc.

de Lima, J. A. (2003). Trained for isolation: the impact of departmental cultures on student teachers' views and practices of collaboration. *Journal of Education for Teaching*, 29 (3), 197– 218.

Farrell, T. S. C. (2003). Learning to teach English language during the first year: personal influences and challenges. *Teaching and Teacher Education*, 19, 95–111.

Farrell, T. S. C. (2006). The first year of language teaching: Imposing order. *System*, 34, 211–21.

Flores, M. A. and Day, C. (2006). Contexts which shape and reshape new teachers' identities: A multi-perspective study. *Teaching and Teacher Education*, 22, 219–32.

Gillham, B. (2000). *The Research Interview*. London: Continuum.

Hebert, E. and Worthy, T. (2001). Does the first year of teaching have to be a bad one? A case study of success. *Teaching and Teacher Education*, 17, 897–911.

Huberman, M. (1993). *The Lives of Teachers* (J. Neufeld, Trans.). London: Cassell and New York: Teachers College Press.

Johnson, K. E. (1996). The vision versus the reality: the tensions of the TESOL practicum. In Freeman, D. and Richards, J. C. (Eds) *Teacher Learning in Language Teaching* (pp. 30–49). Cambridge: Cambridge University Press.

Kelchtermans, G. and Ballet, K. (2002). The micropolitics of teacher induction. A narrative-biographical study on teacher socialisation. *Teaching and Teacher Education*, 18, 105–20.

Kvale, S. (1996). *InterViews: An Introduction to Qualitative Research Interviewing*. Thousand Oaks, CA: Sage.

Lortie, D. C. (1975). *Schoolteacher: A Sociological Study*. Chicago, IL and London: The University of Chicago Press.

Miller, J and Glassner, B. (1997). The 'inside' and the 'outside': Finding realities in interviews. In Silverman, D. (Ed.) *Qualitative Research: Theory Method and Practice* (pp. 99–112). London: Sage Publications Ltd.

Nias, J. (1985). Reference groups in primary teaching: talking, listening and identity. In Ball, S. J. and Goodson, I. F. (Eds) *Teachers' Lives and Careers* (pp. 105–19). Lewes: The Falmer Press.

Office of the National Education Commission. (1999). *National Education Act of BE 2542*. Bangkok, Thailand: Office of the National Education Commission.

Richards, J. C. and Pennington, M. (1998). The first year of teaching. In Richards, J. C. (Ed.) *Beyond Training* (pp. 173–190). Cambridge: Cambridge University Press.

Rogers, D. L. and Babinski, L. M. (2002). *From Isolation to Conversation: Supporting New Teachers' Development*. Albany, NY: State University of New York Press.

Rubin, H. J. and Rubin, I. S. (2005). *Qualitative Interviewing: The Art of Hearing Data*, 2nd edition. Thousand Oaks, CA; Sage Publications Inc.

Ryan, K. (1970). *Don't Smile until Christmas: Accounts of the First Year of Teaching*. Chicago, IL and London: The University of Chicago Press.

Schutt, R. K. (1999). *Investigating the Social World: The Process and Practice of Research*, 2nd edition. Thousand Oaks, CA: Pine Forge Press.

Sikes, P. (1985). The life cycle of the teacher. In Ball, S. J. and Goodson, I. F. (Eds). *Teachers' Lives and Careers* (pp. 27–60). London: Falmer.

So, W. M. M. and Watkins, D. A. (2005). From beginning teacher education to professional teaching: A study of the thinking of Hong Kong primary science teachers. *Teaching and Teacher Education*, 21, 525–41.

Tafa, E. M. (2004). Teacher socialisation; a critical qualitative analysis of the teaching methods of seven new teachers in Botswana junior secondary schools. *International Journal of Educational Development*, 24 (6), 757–8.

Wengraf, T. (2001). *Qualitative Research Interviewing: Biographic Narrative and Semi-structured Methods*. London: Sage Publications Ltd.

6 The transition from teacher education to ESL/EFL teaching in the first year for Non-Native English Speaking Teachers (NNESTs) in Canada

Clea Schmidt

Introduction

New teachers transitioning from teacher education programmes to the ESL/EFL classroom face daunting tasks in their first years of teaching. They have learned about, engaged with, and ideally reflected upon and critiqued various language teaching approaches in their teacher education programmes. Now, with coursework and assignments behind them, they must reconcile what they gleaned from their teacher education with their personal experiences and beliefs about effective language teaching and learning while simultaneously operating within complex sociocultural, administrative, and political contexts (Borg 2003; Kumaravadivelu 2003; 2006; Freeman 2002). And while pre-service language teachers typically work with students in a defined practice teaching capacity, with the transition to the classroom the 'practice' part is over and the numerous demands and responsibilities of the profession manifest with regularity and urgency. Addressing the needs of students who approach language study with a variety of attitudes, goals, and motivations looms large as a priority (Day 1993), as does fostering an environment that is inclusive of the range of cultures and beliefs inherent in multilingual classrooms (Coelho 2004). New teachers also frequently cite managing professional relationships with their students, colleagues and administrators as a major concern (Freeman 2002).

Though all new language teachers potentially face difficulty in satisfying these complex demands, such challenges become even more daunting when considering the experiences of non-native English speaking teachers (NNESTs) of ESL/EFL (Braine 1999), and potential challenges they face in their teacher education programmes and professional contexts. In the ELT field, issues surrounding the teacher education and professional induction of NNESTs become particularly salient in light of the fact that many more teachers speak English as a second or additional language than as a first language, yet NNESTs continue to be marginalized in various educational settings (e.g., Amin 2001).

This chapter describes a qualitative study undertaken in a Canadian university's Certificate in the Teaching of English as a Second Language (C-TESL) programme. The research sought to analyse the professional development needs and experiences of NNESTs of ESL/EFL. Using qualitative, critical action research methodology, data were collected in the form of in-depth interviews with five NNESTs at the end of their C-TESL programme in 2005, interviews with four C-TESL instructors experienced in working with NNESTs, focus groups (one with each group of pre-service NNESTs and instructors), and documents in the form of course assignments and C-TESL programme descriptions and policies. Follow-up interviews were then conducted with two of the original five NNEST participants in 2006 who secured ESL/EFL teaching positions following completion of the C-TESL. Findings are presented through emergent themes that illustrate NNESTs' beliefs and experiences with respect to particular challenges, successes, and issues that emerged during the C-TESL and beyond into the first year of teaching ESL/EFL. Finally, implications for teacher education programming are discussed.

Background literature

Given that non-native English speaking teachers (NNESTs) constitute a major source of English teachers globally, challenges and issues faced by NNESTs in ELT are increasingly problematised in the applied linguistics literature (Braine 1999; Canagarajah 1999). While early publications in this area tended to focus on first-person narrative accounts by NNESTs (e.g., TESOL NNEST Caucus newsletter) or terminology concerns (e.g., Davies 1991; Higgins 2003; Rampton 1996), in recent years a growing number of empirical studies have considered the language proficiency and cross-cultural needs of NNESTs (Gagné and Inbar 2003; Lazaraton 2003). Nevertheless, an effective knowledge base of an NNEST-inclusive teacher education programme has yet to be thoroughly delineated (Park 2004), and the construction of difference as deficit (Cummins 2003) continues to disadvantage NNESTs in terms of student and colleague interactions, teacher education experiences and employment opportunities. The experiences of NNESTs in a range of teacher education and teaching contexts need to be further researched to facilitate inclusive and appropriate teacher education programming and smooth transitions to the language classroom. With these objectives in mind, the current study sought to answer the following question:

> What supports can teacher education programmes enact to
> facilitate the teacher education experience and smooth transition
> to the first year of language teaching for NNESTs?

Research methodology

The research involved three contexts: (1) the university teacher education programme context where NNEST candidates completed their C-TESL; (2) an international EFL business context where one NNEST, Yuki, gained employment subsequent to completing the C-TESL; and (3) a Canadian university English for Academic Purposes programme where a second NNEST, Nadejda, gained employment subsequent to completing the C-TESL. The university-based 200-hour C-TESL programme consisted of four core courses, an elective, and a 20-hour observation and practicum component. The increasing popularity of the programme amongst candidates for whom English is an additional language led to the development of an elective course entitled *English for Non-Native Speaking Teachers of ESL*. This course, employing a content-based instruction model (Crandall and Kaufman 2002), used the theme of professionalism as a vehicle for developing NNEST candidates' professional language and culture skills, and provided the forum for recruiting the NNEST research participants. The context in which Yuki taught was a Business English setting in an international publishing company located in a major urban centre in China, Yuki's country of origin. Nadejda had immigrated to Canada from Eastern Europe prior to starting the C-TESL programme, and upon completion of the C-TESL obtained a position in a Canadian university's English for Academic Purposes programme, where she taught academic writing skills to adult learners from a range of disciplines. Additional information about participants is provided later in this section.

Following from critical social scientific (Kincheloe 2004) and interpretive qualitative research (Glesne 1999; Sax and Fisher 2002) approaches, the research employed a critical action research methodology as defined by Kincheloe (1995), in which 'dominant social interests [are] explicitly acknowledged' and the 'research seeks to improve practice' (p. 74). The main research question stemmed from my experience as the instructor of the *English for Non-native Speaker Teachers of ESL* course, and the critical orientation served to further the broad objective of contributing to better professional development conditions for culturally and linguistically diverse teachers in English-language teacher education. To alleviate the conflict of interest in my role as instructor, candidates were not invited to participate in the research until after final grades for the course had been submitted. NNEST candidates' experiences in the course were used as a starting point to explore their professional development needs and programme perceptions mores broadly, first in the form of a two-hour focus group and subsequently in the form of a one- to two-hour follow-up individual interview in which issues arising from the focus group were explored in greater depth.

The invitation to participate was extended to all eight NNEST candidates who took the course during the 2004–2005 academic year; of those, five agreed to participate. General characteristics and background of the NNEST participants are documented in Table 6.1.

The five NNEST participants were contacted the following year to determine: (a) whether they were employed in an ESL/EFL teaching capacity; and (b) if applicable, how their first year of language teaching was progressing. Of the original five, Alex had pursued employment in a field other than ESL, Jan was volunteering in a range of ESL and other language programme contexts, and Farah was transitioning to a new country where her family had settled to start up a business. Nadejda and Yuki were employed as ESL/EFL teachers and I conducted follow-up interviews with them to document their experiences in their first year of formal language teaching. The follow-up interview with Nadejda, employed in Canada, was conducted face-to-face and the follow-up interview with Yuki, employed in China, was conducted electronically.

In addition to documenting NNESTs' perspectives, four experienced C-TESL instructors took part in a focus group and follow-up individual interview. To alleviate the conflict of interest in my role as colleague, the interviews and focus group were conducted by a trained research assistant. The instructors' input provided additional insights into the professional development needs and experiences of NNEST candidates and the C-TESL programme model. The four instructors had a number of common characteristics: all had at least one advanced degree in the field of TESL, most were born in Canada, multilingual, and had

Table 6.1

NNEST Participant (pseudonyms are used)	*Farah*	*Alex*	*Nadejda*	*Jan*	*Yuki*
Gender	Female	Male	Female	Female	Female
Country/ Region of origin	Iran	Hong Kong	Former Soviet Republic	Korea	China
Length of months time in Canada	22 years	18 years	1.5 years	15 years	8
Language expertise (including English)	Bilingual	Multilingual	Multilingual	Bilingual	Bilingual
ESL/EFL-related teaching experience	Less than one year ESL teaching experience, mostly in one-on-one adult tutoring settings	Less than one year ESL teaching experience, mostly in one-on-one adult tutoring settings	10+ years teaching EFL full-time to children and adults in a classroom context	None	None

extensive Canadian and overseas ESL/EFL teaching experience plus one-and-a-half to five years' experience as a C-TESL instructor.

Data analysis involved coding the data for emerging themes and employing the recursive process identified by Huberman and Miles (2001) with respect to reducing data, displaying data, and drawing and verifying tentative conclusions.

Findings

NNESTs and instructors alike seemed satisfied overall with the structure and content of the C-TESL programme and the two NNESTs who subsequently obtained ESL/EFL teaching positions spoke of a number of positive experiences in their new roles. Nevertheless, interview and focus group data revealed a number of recurring issues and interconnected concerns with respect to NNESTs' self-confidence, perceived professional competence, and discrimination in hiring practices. These concerns have implications for teacher education programming and are revisited in the discussion section.

To ensure NNEST participants' voices maintained a central place in the findings (Griffiths 1998; Tuhiwai Smith 1999), I ordered the data excerpts so the NNESTs' perspectives came first under the discussion of each theme, followed by insights from the C-TESL instructors. Each excerpt is situated within the literature and draws on the critical framework informing the study.

NNESTs' self-confidence

The first major theme emerging from the findings addressed the self-confidence of NNEST participants. All five NNESTs spoke of feeling well-supported and comfortable in their actual C-TESL coursework. Many specifically mentioned the cultural sensitivity shown by the C-TESL instructors as a source of empowerment, aligning with the findings of teacher education research in which programmes seek to foster critical praxis amongst NNESTs (Brutt-Griffler and Samimy 1999; Park 2004). It was during classroom teaching encounters (whether they were volunteering, practicum, or paid teaching positions) that confidence became more of an issue, both for NNESTs with prior experience in professional contexts and for those who were new to a professional environment of any kind. Jan, for example, who opted for ESL teaching after being a successful journalist in Korea, had the opportunity to interact with a range of native English speaking peers in volunteer and C-TESL practicum placements. These interactions offered a mixture of supportive and intimidating experiences. In Jan's words:

> The challenges always happened in the classroom. I was the only
> non-native speaker [teaching] in the classroom and so I was very
> intimidated with the surroundings. For example, in front of me I
> had a classmate who was teaching English at [a university] and
> beside me I had another classmate who was teaching English at [a
> community college]. I was very intimidated but mostly they were
> kind and they tried to help me. I could overcome that, kind of, but
> the skill was challenging because my speaking was not good ...
> Anyway, I was supposed to speak up but some of them, I felt that

> some of them [my peers] looked down upon me. (Jan, NNEST
> Interview, April 2005)

Nadejda, an experienced EFL teacher with over 10 years' experience
in Eastern Europe, obtained a full-time position in a university EAP
programme after completing the C-TESL and reported feeling generally
satisfied in her student and collegial relationships. Nevertheless, she
echoed some of the same concerns as Jan in terms of confidence. In
Nadejda's case, however, the issues appeared more likely to stem from
interactions with students than with colleagues:

> These are the holes that are waiting for teachers who are non-
> native English speakers. And especially if you are very confident
> about your strategies, you are on very good terms with your
> students, and you are kind of thinking 'okay, I'm good'. But all of a
> sudden it could be such a situation where they show you, students
> show you, all the time, that you have to keep up with your level
> and you have to improve yourself and you have to learn all the
> time and you don't have any right to ignore all these things and to
> protect yourself by saying 'oh, okay, it's not my first language'.
> (Nadejda, NNEST Interview, November 2006)

Yuki, entirely new to ESL teaching and with limited work experience
from China, also reported some anxiety concerning her interactions with
students. Demonstrating some of the well-documented pedagogical
strengths discussed in the NNEST literature (Byrnes *et al.* 2002;
Canagarajah 1999), Yuki used her initial lack of confidence as a motiva-
tor to take risks in teaching advanced learners. As she articulated:

> I'm not confident to stand in front of [students] because I think I'm
> also an English learner so it's kind of something I deal with for a
> long time. One thing I feel happy about it is I got experience to
> teach advanced students which I never could imagine I could
> teach them but I did feel they learned something from me. It's not
> always how much knowledge I really can give them but it's for the
> experience. In class time I did some activities with them and I just
> let them feel fun about learning. (Yuki, NNEST Interview, Novem-
> ber 2006)

One of the C-TESL instructors, Grace, sheds light on the confidence
issue by discussing the self-awareness she feels NNESTs generally pos-
sess, in contrast to some of the native English speaking teacher candidates in the C-TESL programme. She highlights her concerns about the
discriminatory attitudes she observes in her classes, echoing the concerns of much mainstream teacher education research (e.g., Seidl and

Friend 2002; Tatar and Horenczyk, 2003) about the unpreparedness of some white, monolingual teachers to effectively address the complexities of culturally and linguistically diverse classrooms. As Grace elaborates:

> Frankly my concerns are more with the native speakers. The non-native speakers are only too aware of their own language weaknesses. They're only too hard on themselves. They're incredibly hardworking, they feel somehow that there is some deficit that they have to make up. Whereas, my native speakers, they all think they can teach and they all think they know grammar and they don't. And they're really discriminatory to boot. So normally those are the ones that I really have problems with. (Grace, Instructor Interview, April 2005)

Perceived professional competence

Appearance, workplace culture, and professional expectations all played a role in how NNEST participants felt others perceived them, how they viewed themselves as professionals, and how C-TESL instructors viewed NNEST candidates. As Alex, new to formal ESL teaching with some one-on-one tutoring experience behind him, succinctly noted when recalling the first time he met his practicum class: 'I actually introduced myself and they were kind of surprised that I'm their teacher. They were like … "you look more like a student than as a teacher"' (NNEST Focus Group, June 2005). Alex felt this comment stemmed in part from the fact that many of the students in class were Asian and so was he, reinforcing Amin's (1997) findings that language learners tend to assume a connection between race and linguistic ability, which can ultimately influence their investment in learning English.

Nadejda reflected on the issue of professional competence by discussing the employment barriers she perceives NNESTs face as they transition from teacher education to the classroom. In the following focus group excerpt, she implores her practicum adviser and host teacher to advocate on her behalf to help the field recognise her abilities. Such a role would involve what Brutt-Griffler and Samimy (1999) refer to as 'critical praxis' in which teacher education faculty take an explicit stance in the empowerment of NNESTs as ESL professionals. In her words:

> All I want to see is the teachers who have seen me teaching, if they see the potential with me, I would like them to become kind of like advocate for me, to tell the teaching world outside that 'we

let her start here' because they [potential employers] don't even want to look at us. (Nadejda, NNEST Focus Group, June 2005)

Jan commented on what she perceives as her limitations in terms of familiarity with Canadian workplace culture and communication skills appropriate to that context. These comments stemmed from a discussion in which Jan felt her host teacher had interpreted something she said as rude because she delivered the message so directly. Jan's taking sole responsibility for the misunderstanding reinforces Johnson's (2003) findings that native English speaking teachers' automatic status as linguistic and cultural 'experts' can negatively impact on NNESTs' identities. Jan reports her perceptions as follows:

> During my experience as a volunteer, I had really kind of difficulties because my lack of knowledge about Canadian culture, especially the workplace culture. So I have realized that I am still oriented to Korean workplace culture and my very personal style from my experience is like that. It was kind of a shock to me because I felt I couldn't communicate with other instructors. I'm not talking about teaching methods or [providing] opportunities to students. It's about connecting with your colleagues and peers. (Jan, NNEST Focus Group, June 2005)

The perceived professional identity of NNESTs also surfaced in Grace's comments, in which she discusses how their engagement with her and other classmates is influenced by NNESTs' choice to position themselves as either ESL learners or ESL teachers in the C-TESL courses.

> Intention is very important because if they identify themselves as ESL students or they identify themselves as potential teachers, their place and role in the [C-TESL] classroom changes. If they identify themselves as an ESL student, my first reaction is that a little bit of the air has been deflated from my tires because that's not my intention of coming into the classroom ... If they identify themselves as potential teachers, whether or not their intention is strong and they identify that way in the classroom, then often they're ... engaged by the other classmates and myself more in terms of '... how will your experiences help you in becoming a teacher'. (Grace, Instructor Focus Group, July 2005)

Other C-TESL instructors' views about the professional competence of NNEST candidates ranged from acknowledging potential gaps in NNESTs' teaching repertoire to openly challenging the deficit perspective (Cummins 2003) sometimes associated with cultural and linguistic difference. Jill, an experienced C-TESL instructor, reflected on NNESTs' professional competence as follows:

> Sometimes [NNESTs] need some time to learn to understand the
> kind of teaching I guess [is] most common in Canada, ... by this I
> mean some of them may have taught before in their own country
> and they have quite a bit of education in their second language, a
> lot of English instruction, but they may or may not have been
> exposed to communicative language teaching. So they may have
> a different idea about what an English teacher does when they
> step in front of the class right, so some of them may or may not be
> comfortable running group activities or pair activities if they
> haven't been exposed or they haven't taught that way before but
> I think that's changing. I think language learners are becoming
> more and more savvy, they know, more savvy about how learning
> can happen and what they can get from different types of
> language learning so I think that's changing. (Jill, Instructor
> Interview, June 2005)

Another C-TESL instructor, Sarah, who had a long history with the
programme and with teacher education in general, spoke of the positive dynamic NNEST candidates helped create in the programme and
the important insights NNESTs bring in their transition from ESL learners to ESL teachers:

> Ever since I started teaching in the programme, there has been a
> group of non-native speaking teachers of English which to me,
> adds so much of a different dynamic to the classroom, people who
> have been through the system as a student, who can really
> understand that type of context. (Sarah, Instructor Interview, April
> 2005)

Discrimination and language ownership

Though researchers have long challenged the authority of the native
speaker in language teaching (e.g., Cook 1999; Rampton 1996), and the
successes and strengths of NNEST professionals have been well-documented (Canagarajah 1999; Lazaraton 2003), discrimination and employment barriers specific to NNESTs persist. The following interview excerpt
with Farah, an experienced businesswoman and long-time resident of
Canada, speaks to some of her concerns around being marginalized as
an immigrant despite what she feels to be her high standard of language:

Farah: The immigrants don't do well, they are always not employed or
            you know, they can't make a living out of that because they have
            to compete with people who have English as their own language ...

> the challenges are always there as usual when English is not your
> mother tongue and no matter how many years you are here. Sur-
> prisingly, sometimes you see people making mistakes that you
> don't and they're native speakers … but one of the things that I …
> learned at the [C-TESL] course was that spoken language is OK. To
> me, that was street language. I'm an educated person, I don't speak
> like that because in a lot of countries, that's how you say that you're
> educated. A couple of us classmates, we both had problems with
> this to accept spoken language and say it's OK as an English teacher.

Interviewer: By this you mean informal language that you found others using.

Farah: Yes, yes, yes. We both thought that if we are English teachers, we
              are going to promote good English. We are not going to say 'I'm
              lovin' it'. It's spoken language! As a teacher I'm supposed to say,
              that's wrong. 'Oh, it's OK'! No, it's not OK. This is English! Why are
              you ruining it? (NNEST Interview, April 2005)

Nadejda further elaborates on employment challenges faced by
NNESTs, based on several unsuccessful experiences she had seeking
ESL teaching employment upon her arrival in Canada prior to starting
the C-TESL. In this same interview data, Nadejda reported obtaining
interviews on account of her impressive EFL teaching resume only to
experience an abrupt change in attitude once the interview began and
potential employers heard her speak. The linguistic discrimination she
experienced had the following effect:

> When you feel that some of the surroundings are not very friendly,
> it immediately makes you silent because you feel that you are not
> accepted or probably they [employers] expect to hear something
> from you that really you can't provide. (Nadejda, NNEST Focus
> Group, June 2005)

Nadejda's concerns parallel the issues raised in this second excerpt
from Farah's interview, in which she elaborates on some of the potential barriers faced by NNESTs. These accounts reinforce the inequities
inherent in multilingual contexts described by Heller and Martin-Jones
(2001), in which educational institutions are seen to privilege certain
types of knowledge and social order. Farah explains:

> I think immigrants stay on the other side of the wall, if they are the
> first generation … that's why that invisible wall always stays.
> Because I don't know what I'm doing wrong and I don't know
> what I'm saying wrong but the expression of people I know, this is
> not something I should have said or you know, done … So if I have
> that problem, I'm sure that most people have it too … It hinders

> your ... being comfortable with the environment and you being
> comfortable with who you are because you want to have friends
> and you want to have people who you can benefit from as they
> enrich your lives, you can enrich their lives. But if that invisible
> wall is there, always people interpret you with the expression on
> their face, and then, it is the same as they say, leave your resume
> here, we'll call you. That kind of attitude. You never get called
> back and you never know why. (Farah, NNEST Interview, April
> 2005)

Additional insights about discriminatory attitudes towards NNESTs emerge from particular experiences recounted by Uma, a C-TESL instructor. Though problematic instances in her classes were infrequent, their occurrence did make a lasting impression and helped inform the anti-discriminatory stance Uma feels should be adopted in all C-TESL courses:

> Over my three to four years I've only had two difficulties, and they
> are very clear in my mind, difficulties with native speaking
> students who don't agree that non-native English speakers should
> be English teachers and who have not been open to working with
> them ... They all need to understand about the discrimination and
> disparity in the world involving accent, language, and race. They
> all need to know their role as English teachers in this political
> situation because there is a role for native and non-native speak-
> ers. (Uma, Instructor Interview, April 2005)

Discussion

The findings point to two main issues that need to be prioritised in language teacher education programming to facilitate the professional development and integration of NNESTs: risk-taking and anti-discrimination. Language teaching involves a range of complex knowledge, processes, tasks, and agendas (Kumaravadivelu 2003; 2006), and taking risks in teacher education is crucial to facilitate language teachers' ability to learn to cope with that complexity. In this study, some NNEST participants reported negative consequences of risk-taking that they linked to their cross-cultural communication styles and language. Jan, for example, blamed herself for not being fully acculturated to North American workplace conventions when a misunderstanding ensued after she delivered a direct (blunt) message to a colleague. Nadejda felt less inclined to take risks with her language in front of students after she conveyed the wrong information to a student in response to a grammar-related question that arose during her first year of language teaching in a North American academic setting. An exception to this situation was Yuki, who embraced the opportunity to teach advanced learners despite her initial nervousness.

The study findings raise questions about who can take risks in language teaching and what risks are appropriate to take, a salient issue in light of the profound impact that the first year of language teaching can have in shaping the practices of NNESTs. If NNESTs feel personally and professionally derailed after negative classroom experiences stemming from perceived communication or language challenges, their willingness to take risks can be hindered and their professional development impeded. Teacher education programmes should play a key role in ensuring that NNESTs are encouraged to gain familiarity with various approaches to professional interactions, and have the chance to receive feedback on their language in a safe and supportive environment while they are learning to teach. If they are supported in trying and erring during their initial preparation, challenges faced when they enter the classroom are likely to be less daunting.

The second main implication for language teacher education is the need for anti-discrimination to play a more central role in teacher education programming. Two of the four teacher educator participants, Grace and Uma, expressed concern about native-English speaking teachers' problematic attitudes towards NNESTs. In the reported instances, teacher educators witnessed NNESTs being marginalised by their peers. A troubling contradiction emerges when ESL teachers, who require sensitivity towards their multilingual students, disrespect or undermine their multilingual counterparts. Most ESL/EFL teachers around the globe speak English as an additional language. This reality, coupled with the need for teachers to work respectfully within diverse staffing contexts, must be addressed before language teachers begin their first year in the classroom. Teacher educators have a responsibility to challenge problematic assumptions around who owns English and who has the right to teach it so that diversity and equity are brought to the forefront of ESL/EFL teachers' work, rather than regarded as just another professional complication overwhelmed new professionals must face.

Conclusion

In documenting the experiences and perceptions of NNESTs and their C-TESL instructors, a number of insights were generated with respect to the original question guiding the study: What supports can teacher education programmes enact to facilitate the teacher education experience and smooth transition to the first year of language teaching for NNESTs?

Though NNESTs shared a number of positive experiences stemming from their involvement in the C-TESL programme and their workplace interactions, the research sought to problematise issues related to the professional development and employment of NNESTs to begin to challenge the systemic inequities facing this crucial yet marginalised group of ESL teachers. The research identified a number of key areas of concern for participating NNESTs, including self-confidence, perceived professional competence and discrimination/employment barriers. Findings showed that though self-confidence and perceived professional confidence often posed challenges according to participating NNESTs, the experiences they described also reflected positive developments when a willingness to take risks was evident and when support was offered by culturally sensitive C-TESL instructors. Interview and focus group data consistently pointed to discrimination and employment barriers as a major frustration and challenge for NNESTs.

NNESTs' frustration with discrimination and employment barriers coupled with C-TESL instructors' acknowledgement of the discriminatory attitudes sometimes evident amongst the wider C-TESL population suggest the need for teacher education programmes to play more of an advocacy role in terms of promoting the assets of NNESTs. Support and encouragement provided for NNESTs with the framework of teacher education programmes and courses is a positive start but teacher educators must also explicitly challenge systemic barriers to the successful integration of NNESTs in the ESL/EFL teaching profession.

References

Amin, N. (2001). Marginalization of non-white immigrant women ESL teachers in Canada. *TESOL Matters*, 11 (2), 1–2.

Amin, N. (1997). Race and the identity of the nonnative ESL teacher. *TESOL Quarterly*, 31, 580–3.

Borg, S. (2003). Teacher cognition in language teaching: A review of research on what language teachers think, know, believe, and do. *Language Teaching*, 31, 81–109.

Braine, G. (Ed.). (1999). *Non-native Educators in English Language Teaching*. Mahwah, NJ: Lawrence Erlbaum Associates.

Brutt-Griffler, J. and Samimy, K. (1999). Revisiting the colonial praxis in the postcolonial: Critical praxis for nonnative English speaking teachers in a TESOL programme. *TESOL Quarterly*, 33 (3), 413–31.

Byrnes, H., Crane, C. and Sprang, A. K. (2002). Nonnative teachers teaching at the advanced level: challenges and opportunities. *ADFL Bulletin*, 33 (3), 25–34.

Canagarajah, S. A. (1999). Interrogating the native speaker fallacy: Non-linguistic roots, non-pedagogical results. In G. Braine (Ed.), *Non-native Educators in English Language Teaching* (pp. 77–92). Mahwah, NJ: Lawrence Erlbaum Associates.

Coelho, E. (2004). *Adding English: A Guide to Teaching in Multilingual Classrooms*. Toronto, ON: Pippin Publishing.

Cook, V. (1999). Going beyond the native speaker in language teaching. *TESOL Quarterly*, 33 (2), 185–209.

Crandall, J. and Kaufman, D. (Eds). (2002). *Content-based Instruction in Higher Education Settings*. Alexandria, VA: Teachers of English to Speakers of Other Languages (TESOL), Inc.

Cummins, J. (2003). Challenging the construction of difference as deficit: Where are identity, intellect, imagination, and power in the new regime of truth? In P. Trifonas (Ed.), *Pedagogies of Difference: Rethinking Education for Social Change* (pp. 41–60). London: Routledge.

Davies, A. (1991). *The Native Speaker in Applied Linguistics*. Edinburgh: Edinburgh University Press.

Day, R. (1993). Models and the knowledge base of second language teacher education. *University of Hawai'i Working Papers in ESL*, 11 (2), 1–13.

Freeman, D. (2002). The hidden side of the work: Teacher knowledge and learning to teach. *Language Teaching*, 35, 1–13.

Gagné, A. and Inbar, O. (2003). *Language Proficiency Development of Non-native English-speaking Teacher Candidates: A Comparative Case Study of Two Teacher Preparation Programmes in Canada and Israel*. TESOL Priority Research Grant.

Glesne, C. (1999). *Becoming Qualitative Researchers*. New York, NY: Addison Wesley Longman, Inc.

Griffiths, M. (1998). *Educational Research for Social Justice: Getting off the Fence*. Buckingham, UK: Open University Press.

Heller, M. and Martin-Jones, M. (2001). *Voices of Authority: Education and Linguistic Difference*. Westport, CT: Ablex Publishing.

Higgins, C. (2003). 'Ownership' of English in the outer circle: an alternative to the NS-NNS dichotomy. *TESOL Quarterly*, 37 (4), 615–44.

Huberman, A. M. and Miles, M. B. (2001). Data management and analysis methods. In C. F. Conrad, J. G. Haworth, L. R. Lattuca (Eds), *Qualitative Research in Higher Education: Expanding Perspectives* (pp. 553–71). New York, NY: Pearson.

Johnson, K. A. (2003). Professional development of an NEST through working alongside an NNEST. *NNEST Newsletter*, 5 (2), 10–16.

Kincheloe, J. (1995). Meet me behind the curtain: The struggle for a critical postmodern action research. In P. L. McLaren and J. M. Giarelli (Eds), *Critical Theory and Educational Research* (pp. 71–89). New York, NY: SUNY Press.

Kincheloe, J. (2004). The knowledges of teacher education: Developing a critical complex epistemology. *Teacher Education Quarterly*, 31 (1), 49–66.

Kumaravadivelu, B. (2006). *Understanding Language Teaching: From Method to Postmethod.* Mahwah, NJ: Lawrence Erlbaum Associates.

Kumaravadivelu, B. (2003). *Beyond Methods: Macrostrategies for Language teaching.* New Haven, CT: Yale University Press.

Lazaraton, A. (2003). Incidental displays of cultural knowledge in the nonnative-English speaking teacher's classroom. *TESOL Quarterly*, 37 (2), 213–45.

Park, G. (2004). A call for preparing all teachers: TESOL standards for NNES teacher candidates. *TEIS News*, 19 (2), 5–7.

Rampton, M. B. H. (1996). Displacing the 'native speaker': expertise, affiliation, and inheritance. In T. Hedge and N. Whitney (Eds), *Power, Pedagogy, and Practice* (pp. 17–42). Oxford: Oxford University Press.

Seidl, B. and Friend, G. (2002). Leaving authority at the door: equal-status community-based experiences and the preparation of teachers for diverse classrooms. *Teaching and Teacher Education*, 18, 421–33.

Sax, C. and Fisher, D. (2002). Using qualitative action research to effect change: Implications for professional education. *Teacher Education Quarterly*, 28 (2), 71–80.

Tatar, M. and Horenczyk, G. (2003). Diversity-related burnout amongst teachers. *Teaching and Teacher Education*, 19, 397–408.

Tuhiwai Smith, L. (1999). *Decolonizing Methodologies: Research and Indigenous Peoples.* London, UK: Zed Books Ltd.

7 The beliefs and practices of novice teachers in Hong Kong: change and resistance to change in an Asian teaching context

Alan W. Urmston and Martha C. Pennington

Introduction

In the summer of 1997, the cohort of student teachers graduating from the BA in Teaching English (BATESL) at the City University of Hong Kong found themselves about to enter the workforce at a critical time in the Territory's history, as its sovereignty was being returned to China. For them, there were more immediate concerns than the changeover; those that had chosen to become teachers were looking to enter the teaching profession in order to put into action what they had learned during the previous three years. This chapter looks at the experiences of a sample of these new teachers in the two-year period following their graduation, i.e. from July 1997 to the summer of 1999. The study provided indications of the extent of lasting influence of the BATESL course on its graduates and how their beliefs and practices evolved during their first two years as graduates/novice teachers.

Background literature

Why novice teachers often diverge from best practices

It seems that most student teachers believe that no amount of teaching methodology taught in an education college or university department can match what they learn from experience as teachers (and students) themselves and in real teaching situations (Ethell and McMeniman 2000;

Freeman 1991). This suggests that the reality of the classroom situation will have more effect on their approach to teaching than will the philosophies, methods and techniques to which they are exposed during their formal course work. As former students of the secondary school system, those pursuing a qualification aimed at secondary school teaching are well aware of the environment in which they will have to teach and the approaches they believe are likely to be effective in it. The question to be answered is whether their formal preparation for teaching can in any way change the fundamental beliefs they have regarding which approaches would be both successful and practical.

Practicality has been shown to be the major concern of pre-service teachers. For this group, practicality generally involves the two key factors of maintaining discipline and motivating students (Stuart and Thurlow 2000). In order to accomplish the first of these goals, although novice teachers are aware of its purported drawbacks in terms of motivation, direct instruction is most often employed as it ensures teacher control (Galton 2000). For the second of these goals, novices are 'inclined to believe that there exists somewhere a set of guidelines, or even tips, which will enable them to survive as teachers no matter what the context of their teaching' (Galton 2000: 5). While they may not feel that they can adopt a particular pedagogical framework, such as communicative, interpretative or other innovative approaches, they will look for specific lesson plans or activities which they think will motivate their students while at the same time allowing them to maintain discipline. In a study of five of the graduates from the first cohort of the BATESL course at the City University of Hong Kong in their first year as qualified teachers, Pennington and Richards (1997) discovered that once they were in the classroom, the teachers diverged significantly from the communicative, process-oriented principles and practices emphasised on the course. In terms of changes to teachers' pedagogical frameworks, the teachers underwent a *regression to context* in that they were oriented to the transmissive, product approaches of the Hong Kong educational context and the need to cover the prescribed syllabus while also devoting considerable attention to establishing and maintaining discipline in what were often difficult teaching conditions.

Pennington and Richards (1997) pinpointed a number of possible reasons why these novice teachers, fresh from their course of training, failed to apply what they had been taught. First, the different cultures and backgrounds of their instructors on the BATESL course (expatriates with little experience of the Hong Kong teaching culture as well as Hong Kong Chinese with both overseas and local experience) led to inconsistencies in teaching philosophy and a lack of as strong an emphasis on communicative approaches as the course developers had envisaged. Second, the teachers' prior experiences as students within the highly examination-driven, product-oriented educational system – like the system itself of which they are a part, which has failed to incorporate significant process and communicative innovations in spite of considerable efforts in the past 30 years on the part of the educational system to do so – proved more resistant to change than had been expected. Third, the influences on the teachers during their practice teaching – i.e. supervising teachers, panel chairs (heads of department) and other colleagues – served to reinforce the teaching norms and discourage innovative, 'alternative' approaches as being too risky and diverting attention away from the crucial goal of preparing the students for examinations. Fourth, the overwhelming constraints of the system, such as heavy workload, large class size and students' low English proficiency and motivation meant that, given their inexperience and lack of confidence, they were unable and unwilling to venture beyond their own past experience as students and the safety of what they were expected (by their students, panel chair and their teachers) to do. Finally, their nearness in age to their students meant that they could sympathise with them in terms of the difficulties they (students and teachers) were facing in learning and using English, resulting in conflicting perceptions of their roles as teachers and near-peers as well as in use of the mother tongue for support.

As Freeman and Johnson (1998) put it: 'language teaching cannot be understood apart from the sociocultural environments in which it takes place and the processes of establishing and navigating social values in which it is embedded' (p. 409). Therefore, a description of the sociocultural environment as it exists in Hong Kong schools is necessary to put any process of change and resistance to change into context.

A tough place to be innovative: The Hong Kong educational context

Hong Kong teachers generally have to cope with large classes and a lack of encouragement to experiment with innovative teaching methods (Pennington 1995). They teach under an extremely heavy schedule and paper-marking load, and they must cover a required syllabus densely packed with points of language and assignments. It is undisputed that Hong Kong has long had an educational culture which is a textbook case of transmissive,[1] teacher-centred, examination-based practices

(Pennington 1995; Young and Lee 1987) which are framed within traditional, Chinese principles of control and respect for authority (Pennington and Cheung 1995; So 1992).

In terms of English teaching, the Education Bureau (formerly the Education and Manpower Bureau) have introduced various initiatives aimed at improving education and modernising instructional practices and the educational culture. These include the employment of expatriate, native-speaking English teachers (NETs); changes in the English teaching curriculum to reflect modern developments in ESL; and a tightening of the requirements for teachers of English in schools, including the statutory Language Proficiency Requirement (LPR).[2] In the past, a reasonable proficiency in the English language was considered a sufficient qualification for teaching English in Hong Kong secondary schools but during the 1990s this situation changed noticeably. Expansions in the tertiary education sector as a result of substantial government investment led to an increase in the provision of English language teacher education courses. The majority of Hong Kong's tertiary institutes offer Bachelor and Masters degrees in areas of Applied Linguistics or Teaching English as a Second Language. The BA course in Teaching English as a Second Language (BATESL) of the City University of Hong Kong was launched in 1991, with the following aims:

> Graduates of the BATESL program are … expected to be comfortable teaching according to the principles of communicative language teaching, while at the same time being able to adapt their teaching to student expectations and to the type of class they are teaching. They are also expected to be able to interpret what they have learned flexibly based on their own judgement.
> (Pennington *et al.* 1996: 19)

The novice teacher participants of the study described here all graduated from the BATESL in 1997.

Research methodology

The data for the case studies came from interviews and lesson observations with novice teachers as summarised in Table 7.1.

In August 1998, five BATESL graduates were interviewed one year after graduation to ascertain their progress as teachers and their views in retrospect on education and the BATESL course. In the interviews, the teachers were asked for their reflections on the BATESL course,

Table 7.1

Date	Data collection method	Summary of process
August 1998	Interview	Five BATESL graduates were interviewed in two separate sessions, one year after graduating from the course.
May/June 1999	Lesson observation and interview	Three of the BATESL graduates were observed (twice) in their teaching environments, two years after graduation.

their practice teaching experience and their experience post-graduation. The interviews were transcribed and the transcriptions analysed qualitatively for key points by the constant comparative method.[3] Approximately one year later, in May/June 1999, two of the group, John and Dorothy, along with another graduate from the same cohort, Ka Man, were observed while teaching in their schools.[4] The lesson observations were intended to be a small-scale follow-up study to an earlier questionnaire and interview study.[5] Each of the teachers was observed twice in his/her classroom. During the observations, a detailed record was taken of the teacher's instructional procedures, student behaviours, teacher-student interactions, and teacher and student language use. Each observation was immediately followed by an individual interview to elicit the observed teachers' reflections on the lesson just taught and on their general teaching situation, and comments were added by the observer as to whether the teacher's reflections corresponded to or contradicted the observed behaviours. The three teachers and their teaching situations are now described.[6]

John

After graduation, John worked in the English Department at the City University of Hong Kong as a research assistant for one year. He had been working in his current school since September 1998. The school was privately run and offered courses mainly for students who wished to improve the HKCEE (Hong Kong Certificate of Education Examination) or A Level grades that they had gained in secondary school. They could also study vocational courses such as business, hotel management and design, as well as core A Level Use of English and Chinese Language and Culture (the language qualifications required for entry to higher education in Hong Kong).

Two separate lessons were observed on the same day in May 1999. The first was with a Use of English group, who were asked to brainstorm ideas for speaking practice activities through which they planned to improve their English during the summer vacation. The second lesson involved the teacher giving feedback to students on their written assignments.

Dorothy

The teacher had spent her first year after graduation in 1997 working in another field (hotel and tourism) and so was in her first year in the school at the time of the observation. She would not be staying on at the school after her contract expired at the end of the current school year. The school was a Band Four/Five[7] government-aided co-educational secondary school in a new town in the New Territories. In each cycle of six days students had nine English lessons plus one from the NET, which would be used for speaking practice.

Two classes were observed on the same day in May 1999. The first class observed was a Form 2 class of about 40 students. In the lesson, Dorothy prepared the students to write a composition about pandas. In the second observation, Dorothy administered an oral examination to a class of 30 Form 3 students. Dorothy sat at the teacher's desk and the students came out to the teacher's desk in pairs to read a short dialogue that they had prepared in advance.

Ka Man

Ka Man had been teaching at the school as a supply (substitute) teacher from November 1998 and had been employed as a replacement for a NET who had not taken up employment at the school. She had spent one year in the UK studying for an MBA after graduating from the BATESL course in 1997. She intended to remain at the school on a permanent contract from September 1999.

The school was new, having been open for only three years. At the time of the observation, there were Form 1 and 2 classes (grades 7 and 8) and Form 4 and 5 classes (grades 10 and 11). The school was described by the teacher as a Band Three or Four Chinese-medium (CMI) secondary school in a new town in Kowloon.

In addition to their English class, the students were required to attend an *English Enhancement Scheme* that took place over three or four mornings during school holidays. In this scheme they took part in activities using only English. The scheme was described by Ka Man as a

Government initiative for CMI schools for which the school received funding.

The first class observed was a 'split-class' group of 14 Form 1 students. It was the policy of the school to divide Form 1 English classes into smaller groups for all but one class of the ten in the teaching cycle. Ka Man described the students as being of quite high ability but weak in English. In the lesson observed, the class did work on asking and answering *wh*-questions.

In the second observation, three days later, the class was a complete one of about 35 students, some of them the same as those in the previous observation. Ka Man explained that the students lacked interest in English and that some were unwilling to participate in class activities. In the lesson observed, the students worked from the textbook on identifying parts of the body. They had already done some preliminary work on this in the previous lesson.

Findings

What was learned in interviews with participants one year after graduation

Reflecting on their practice teaching during the BATESL course, the graduates agreed that the period of the practice was too short. However, most felt that it had been worthwhile and had given them the opportunity to try a few of the teaching practices that they had learned. There was some disagreement over whether the high degree of examination-orientation prevalent in Hong Kong education was attributable more to students or teachers. The consensus was that Hong Kong society is achievement-oriented and this is reflected in schools, with teachers feeling that they had to 'teach to the test' and that students were only interested in learning in order to get higher grades. John and Dorothy exchanged views on this:

John I don't know, maybe in lower forms, maybe you can teach in a more interactive mode, but in upper forms, the Form 4 or above, less interactive. Maybe because the teacher just gives them some mock papers to do, how can it be interactive? I'm not sure.

Dorothy Well I agree with John, basically the trend is like that and for senior form students, if you use some interactive approaches, they will

> say that you are wasting the time. So it's a norm, I can say it's a norm.

In sum, both teachers and students were seen as being locked into a transmissive, ends-driven system of teaching and learning. The domination of examinations was felt in terms of teaching approach, as the graduates believed that it was difficult to adopt interactive or innovative approaches with higher level students who would expect examination practice, while on the other hand lower level students might not have the proficiency required to engage in communicative activities.

There was evidence of the lasting influence of the BATESL course on the graduates when describing their teaching style. At least three of the graduates expressed confidence in their ability to put their training into action, while also showing awareness of the realities of the classroom and the need to modify the approaches they had learned. According to Dorothy:

Dorothy   Yes I am [confident] … I have been to a range of schools and they are Band 3 and Band 1 students and even [though] they are in different bandings, I can communicate with them and I can give them different level[s] of knowledge based on their proficiency.

They stressed the importance of understanding the needs of students and forming good relationships with them, at the same time seeking to differentiate between having a good teacher–student relationship and trying to become 'friends' with the students. Again, Dorothy had something to say on this:

Dorothy   Maybe students have to respect you, at least in the classroom, and out of the classroom they can be very friendly with you. It seems that this problem can be solved but it's hard to control. You can't tell them, "Now you have to respect me," even if you give them an explanation, they may not be able to follow.

The graduates were positive about the BATESL course and most felt that they had learned valuable language and teaching skills. They also remarked that being at the university with other students had helped them increase their confidence in terms of personality and social relationships – an effect of higher study that has not generally been noted in the literature but which has positive implication for teaching. As John remarked:

John   But during the BATESL course I realised that … actually sometimes human relationships is a friendship and also our attitudes towards

> different kinds of things may change the result, so during the
> BATESL course I learned to [have] a rather positive attitude towards
> learning and also towards the social relationships, and I realise that
> I met a lot of good friends and I improved myself. At least I [now]
> have enough confidence to organise various activities on my own.

They believed that the modifications to their teaching philosophies and approaches had been caused by the constraints present in the schools in which they had taught during practice teaching or post-graduation. The tendency to cite the constraints in teaching as causing teachers to retreat from what they considered 'best practice' and to restrict their innovativeness was a strong theme that emerged from these case studies and in the related larger studies of this group of trainee teachers (Urmston, 2003).

Participants' practices as revealed through observations and post-observation interviews

Observing some of the teachers in their teaching situations provided more detailed information regarding their practices and approaches than had been acquired from the interviews. Two of the teachers reported having a certain amount of flexibility to supply their own teaching materials but having limited time to spend designing them. In addition, they clearly felt constrained by needing to follow a syllabus and course textbook. John said that as his classes were examination preparation classes, he had limited scope to introduce anything innovative. He said that he did try to introduce group work wherever possible for speaking practice. In one of the observed lessons, he attempted to form the students into groups so that they could share ideas on language learning activities, although there did not appear to be much genuine communication occurring in the target language. All three teachers felt that they were constrained by the proficiency of the students they were teaching as well as by the need to cater to the students' product-oriented aims. They reported having limited opportunities to adopt communicative or innovative practices as a result. Differences in the three teachers' observed and reported approaches were generally attributed to the level and/or age of the students they were teaching. There was also evidence of the teachers regarding themselves as innovators within their schools and among their colleagues, possibly as a result of their background of the BATESL and their relatively fresh views on teaching compared to their more experienced colleagues. This apparent innovativeness was not particularly evident during the lessons observed, although Ka Man did make good use of a variety of techniques to generate interest in her students.

Discussion

It would appear to be a common factor that teachers in Hong Kong schools, particularly new teachers, overstate the impact of constraints within the system as preventing innovation. Interacting with the system is the norm in all teaching situations, especially in public education. With these teachers, the constraints within the educational system and the students' ability and/or language proficiency were consistently cited as the main reasons for the lack of successful diffusion and adoption of educational innovations. It can be observed that these constraints and limitations are an aspect of the norms of the system and the user population, and that innovations will be diffused to a degree dependent on how they interact with these factors (Rogers, 1995). The tendency seems to be for new teachers to be at the same time overly idealistic in their expectations and overly pessimistic about their options. These factors may result in some of them (such as some of the BATESL graduates) either not entering teaching after graduation or else soon leaving the profession when their expectations are not met.

In general, the teachers felt that their relationships with their colleagues were good and that they could rely on them for support and guidance. There was no indication of the commonly reported isolationism experienced by Hong Kong teachers (Fung 2000; Lam *et al.* 2002; Morris 1995). On the other hand, these three novice teachers did not place much emphasis on such relationships and may have regarded them as 'good' within the limited expectations of what they should be within the norms of Hong Kong educational contexts. The teachers' relationships with the students were also described as good. Dorothy and Ka Man reported that they were able to forge better relationships with the lower form students than those of the higher forms. John was teaching in a post-secondary school and so all of his students were of Form 4 or above. All three teachers seemed, from the evidence of the observations, to have developed good working relationships with their students, although it was difficult to judge whether these relationships extended to the point where the students might approach the teacher outside of class for consultation or simply to be friendly. John did report that he met with students outside of class. John, who was teaching only students in the higher forms, was able to form good relationships with these older students whereas Dorothy and Ka Man found it more difficult to teach students in the higher forms than in the lower forms. Each of the teachers had been given a number of responsibilities and was involved in numerous extra-curricular activities, consistent with the government's policy of increased English language support through activities for students in CMI schools.

The teachers expressed mixed views concerning their teaching situation at the time of the observations. John and Ka Man seemed reasonably content with what they were doing, expressing some frustration with students' attitudes and lack of motivation, while at the same time feeling that they were doing a good job and were gaining valuable experience. Only Dorothy was wholly negative in her appraisal of her situation. She felt that it would have been better for her to be teaching higher form students, as she would be better able to communicate with them, despite the fact that she had earlier admitted to having better relations with the lower form than the higher form students. She seemed to accept the fact that new teachers are generally given primarily lower form students to teach and that the higher forms, which mainly focus on examination preparation, are taken by the more experienced teachers. She was also disappointed at what she saw as the necessity of using mainly Cantonese in her lessons, which contradicted her beliefs about teaching. Dorothy and also John, but to a lesser extent, expressed their frustration with having to 'teach to the syllabus', citing the constraints of having to cover language items in the set syllabus as restricting the possibilities for being innovative in terms of teaching approach. They seemed not to have been able to separate the content or design of instruction from approach and procedure (Richards and Rodgers, 1982) and not to have considered ways they could adopt their own teaching style while still covering the items on the syllabus. The repeated theme of regarding the syllabus as a barrier to the use of innovative approaches, rather than as the framework within which to use such approaches, is evident here, as is the tendency to blame external factors for teachers' restricted practices that might in reality be partly under their own control. Like other novice teachers, these Hong Kong teachers did not feel empowered to own their decision-making in the teaching contexts.

One of the most noticeable aspects of the observations was the degree of inconsistency demonstrated by the teachers. This was manifested in two ways: there was inconsistency between their reported behaviour and their observed practices, and there was inconsistency in their beliefs. An example of the former type of inconsistency was in the view of Ka Man, who said she was not able to adopt communicative practices, but in fact did so during her lessons. An example of the latter type of inconsistency was the statement by Dorothy that she would prefer to teach higher form students, as she felt she would be able to communicate better with them; but then she also said she had better relations with the lower form students. It could be that these novice teachers had not yet developed consistent teaching views or frameworks which interpreted the various factors that affected their teaching into a consistent perspective. These contradictions could also be indicative of a more widespread inconsistency between beliefs and practices and a lack of integration of perspectives within the Hong Kong teaching context more generally, which would have been particularly acute during such a period of change as existed in the period of the handover.

Conclusion

A key area to emerge from this study of novice teachers was the potential for adopting innovative approaches. The influence of parents and society on the approaches and procedures adopted in the classroom was felt keenly by the teachers observed as the educational system remained examination-driven. The novice teachers studied regarded themselves as innovators within their schools, in comparison with colleagues who had been teaching for some years and who had developed set routines for teaching. The teachers felt that their BA course had given them the background in teaching that they needed and the predisposition to be innovative in their teaching. At the same time, they found that the culture in the schools in which they were teaching was frequently not conducive to innovation as pressure to conform to the syllabus was high. This was especially true for students in the higher forms, those of Form 4 and above, who were being prepared for external examinations. Being inexperienced teachers, they felt a great deal of frustration, as they believed it was only possible to use innovative procedures or techniques with the higher form students if those students had the ability and maturity to take advantage of them, which they often did not. Although teachers generally had more freedom to teach lower form students using their own methods, the teachers did not have enough experience to be successful in guiding students to be able to perform the tasks that the teachers wanted them to perform. They thought it likely that they would be able to experiment more in their teaching as they became more experienced and their authority within the school increased. It seems to be a characteristic of teachers in Hong Kong to put off doing something perceived to be difficult or even controversial, looking ahead to some time in the future when conditions will be better (Pennington 1998).

As Pennington (1998) notes, this form of *unreality* seems to be a feature of Hong Kong people in general and is perhaps related to the characterisations of Hongkongers as being conservative towards change and not wishing to act, even though they may see the need to do so.[8] Hence, the reality might be that teachers would continually put off introducing innovative practices into their teaching, citing the constraints of the system as working against them and their educational ideals. This point highlights the need for more support for novice teachers in their first year or two in the classroom.

The findings from this study indicate that for Hong Kong teachers new to the profession, the long-standing constraints of heavy workload, large class size and the need to adhere to a syllabus heavily geared towards standardising instruction and preparing students for internal and external assessment had been compounded during the immediate post-handover period by increasing pressure to perform coming from school administrators, parents and the government. At this time, with a large number of changes taking place, teachers – both experienced and novice – simply had to cope. With limited support or sympathy, and with pressure to conform to the conservative educational culture working against any desire and ability to be original or to innovate, they were caught in the middle. The message seems to be that there was a need to address these teachers' concerns and constraints if any innovative practices or planned educational reforms were to succeed. Their concerns and constraints having remained unaddressed, these newly graduated teachers, like so many others before them, instead of infusing new ideas and practices into the educational system were largely absorbed into its traditions.

Notes

1. Using the terminology of Barnes and Shemilt (1974), who defined a polarity of teaching in terms of practices centred either on transmission or interpretation of information.
2. Since September 2003, all new entrants to the profession have been required to attain the LPR for English language proficiency and pedagogical

content knowledge. Serving English teachers have had to do so since 2005. Teachers can attain the LPR by virtue of having a relevant first degree and teacher training qualification or by taking the Language Proficiency Assessment for Teachers (LPAT).

3.   A listing of the main points emerging from these interviews as well as the full transcriptions can be found in Urmston (2003).

4.   Not their real names.

5.   As reported in Urmston (2003).

6.   For a more detailed account of the classes observed and the follow-up interviews, see Urmston (2003).

7.   The 'banding' of a secondary school refers to the way in which students graduating from primary schools were ranked according to results obtained in the Territory-wide Academic Aptitude Test (AAT). Those in the top band were able to choose which secondary school they wished to apply for first. Therefore, the so-called Band 1 schools, which were generally the well-established and English-medium schools, invariably had the best intake of students. The lower band schools, such as the one where Dorothy worked, in contrast, would have students with limited English and general academic skills and, as compared to the higher bands schools, additional motivation and discipline problems. The system has since been overhauled and the AAT abolished in favour of a more comprehensive approach to secondary school intake.

8.   This unreality is often demonstrated in student compositions and letters to the editor of local newspapers which, after addressing some social or environmental problem, will invariably finish with a phrase such as 'I hope that this problem can be solved in the future'.

References

Barnes, D. and Shemilt, D. (1974). Transmission and interpretation. *Educational Review*, 26, 213–28.

Ethell, R. G. and McMeniman, M. M. (2000). Unlocking the knowledge in action of an expert practitioner. *Journal of Teacher Education*, 51 (2), 87–101.

Falvey, P. and Coniam, D. (1997). Introducing English language benchmarks for Hong Kong teachers: A preliminary overview. *Curriculum Forum*, 6 (2), 16–35.

Freeman, D. and Johnson, K. E. (1998). Reconceptualizing the knowledge-base of language teacher education. *TESOL Quarterly*, 32 (3), 397–417.

Freeman, D. (1991). 'Mistaken constructs': Re-examining the nature and assumptions of language teacher education. In J. E. Alatis (Ed.), *Linguistics and Language Pedagogy: The State of the Art*. Georgetown University Round Table on Languages and Linguistics (pp. 25–39). Washington, DC: Georgetown University Press.

Fung, Y. (2000). A constructivist strategy for developing teachers for change: A Hong Kong experience. *Journal of In-Service Education,* 26 (1), 153–67.

Galton, M. (2000). Two decades of change in English teacher education: The consequences of neglecting educational theory. *Asia-Pacific Journal of Teacher Education and Development,* 2 (2), 1–10.

Lam, S. F., Yim, P. S. and Lam, W. H. (2002). Transforming school culture: Can true collaboration be initiated? *Educational Research,* 44 (2), 181–95.

Morris, P. (1995). *The Hong Kong School Curriculum: Development, Issues and Policies.* Hong Kong: Hong Kong University Press.

Pennington, M. C. (1995). *Eight Case Studies of Classroom Discourse in the Hong Kong Secondary English Class.* Research Report No. 42. Department of English, City University of Hong Kong.

Pennington, M. C. (1998). Perspectives on language use in Hong Kong at century's end. In M. C. Pennington (Ed.), *Language in Hong Kong at Century's End* (pp. 3–4). Hong Kong: Hong Kong University Press.

Pennington, M. C. and Cheung, M. (1995). Factors shaping the introduction of process writing in Hong Kong secondary schools. *Language, Culture and Curriculum,* 8 (1), 15–34.

Pennington, M. C. and Richards, J. C. (1997). Re-orienting the teaching universe: The experience of five first-year English teachers in Hong Kong. *Language Teaching Research,* 1 (2), 149–78.

Pennington, M. C., Richards, J. C., Urmston, A. W. and Lee, Y. P. (1996). *Learning to Teach English in Hong Kong: The First Year in the Classroom.* Research Monograph No. 13, Department of English, City University of Hong Kong.

Richards, J. C. and Rodgers, T. S. (1982). Method: Approach, design, procedure. *TESOL Quarterly,* 16, 153–68.

Rogers, E. M. (1995). *Diffusion of Innovations.* Fourth Edition. New York: Free Press.

So, D. (1992). Language-based bifurcation of secondary education in Hong Kong: Past, present and future. In K. K. Luke (Ed.), *Into the Twenty-first Century: Issues of Language Education in Hong Kong* (pp. 69–95). Hong Kong: Linguistic Society of Hong Kong.

South China Morning Post. (2000). Teachers vow to boycott test. *South China Morning Post* 28 May.

Stuart, C. and Thurlow, D. (2000). Making it their own: Preservice teachers' experiences, beliefs, and classroom practices. *Journal of Teacher Education,* 51 (2), 113–21.

Urmston, A. W. (2003). Learning to teach English in Hong Kong: effects of the changeover in sovereignty. Unpublished PhD Thesis. University of Luton.

Young, R. and Lee, S. (1987). EFL curriculum innovation and teachers' attitudes. In R. Lord and N. L. Cheng (Eds), *Language Education in Hong Kong* (pp. 83–98). Hong Kong: Chinese University Press.

8 Teaching post-CELTA: the interplay of novice teacher, course and context

Michaela Borg

Introduction

Much has been written of the complexity of the process of becoming a teacher, from the interplay between experience and the course to the process of socialisation of the novice in the school culture. Many of these studies have been carried out in a general education context rather than with TESOL professionals and training specifically. There are many useful lessons which we can take from this research but we must also recognise that the situation of TESOL is very diverse including work in a range of settings from primary and secondary schools in a state system to universities, to private language schools. The teachers and learners involved in these different settings are also very diverse, varying in backgrounds, experience, age, etc.

This chapter focuses on one group of teachers, native English speaking teachers who undertook a four week initial teacher training certificate (Certificate in English Language Teaching to Adults) and then went on to work in teaching English in a variety of settings. Some of the issues raised in this case study will be particular to this group of expatriate novice teachers, other issues will be relevant to novices entering a new English teaching context. Despite the importance of the CELTA course for British English Language Teaching professionals, there has been a distinct lack of research into the course and its impact on novice teachers (Ferguson and Donno 2003). And, whilst it is commonly asserted that the course is highly effective, this has not been systematically established.

Background literature

The CELTA course was previously know as the CTEFLA (Certificate in Teaching English as a Foreign Language to Adults) and is an initial teacher training qualification for teaching English as a Foreign Language. It is an important gate-keeping qualification in the British English Language Teaching industry, accepted worldwide by employers. More than 900 CELTA courses are run each year in the 286 centres covering 54 countries (University of Cambridge 2006). Recent figures from UCLES suggest that each year approximately 10,000 people complete the course.

The range of people who undertake a CELTA course, and their expectations and motivations, are likely to be quite different to people who undertake longer teacher education courses such as Bachelor's degree in Education or a Master's degrees. Britain has a strong tradition of people going abroad and supporting themselves as English language teachers. A significant proportion of people who undertake a CELTA intend to travel abroad for a year or two and finance their travel by teaching. On the official University of Cambridge CELTA website, under the heading 'who is CELTA for?', they list the following: people who want a career in ELT; people who want to change careers; people who are teaching without formal qualifications; and people who want to work in Further, Adult and Community Education in England and Wales. Of the individuals who leave Britain each year to teach overseas, it is estimated that 90 per cent have a Certificate from either the University of Cambridge or its major competitor, Trinity College, London (Gray 2000).

The University of Cambridge Exam board who oversee the CELTA specify:

- the course aims, which enable candidates to:

  - acquire essential subject knowledge and familiarity with the principles of effective teaching;

  - acquire a range of practical skills for teaching English to adult learners;

  - demonstrate their ability to apply their learning in a real teaching context;

- the minimum number of hours for the course and areas to be covered, 120 hours contact to include:

  - input;

- supervised lesson planning;

- 6 assessed hours of teaching practice;

- feedback on teaching;

- peer observation;

- a minimum 6 hours of observation of experienced teachers;

- and tutorial time.

- there is also an additional requirement for candidates to undertake a minimum of 80 hours of reading, preparation, assignments etc.

The qualification is practical with theory being kept to a minimum, a practice justified by the idea that the Certificate is intended to be followed by 'on the job' support and by further teacher training later in a teacher's career: the Diploma or DELTA – minimum two years' experience required; and possibly a Master's – usually two years' experience required (in the UK). In reality few teachers undertake further training or education and hence the Certificate retains an even more central role in the world of ELT. It is not simply *the* gateway into the profession, but in many cases it may also be the only qualification a teacher undertakes. Roberts (1998) estimates that only 10 per cent of teachers take a diploma course, although this information needs to be kept in perspective: approximately 50–70 per cent of people entering TESOL leave the profession within three to five years (Phillips, 1989).

From its conception, the course rationale carried an explicit expectation that training would continue, post-course, in the novice teachers' place of employment: 'those who did well on the course would teach mainly abroad for a year or two as virtual apprentices before becoming fully professional teachers' (Haycraft 1988: 9). The most recent revision of the course has reemphasised its introductory nature, regardless of grade achieved, and it is not uncommon to refer to CELTA graduates as 'TEFL-*initiated*' rather than 'TEFL-*qualified*' (Lewis 2001).

Pass	'They will continue to need guidance to help them to develop and broaden their range of skills as teachers in post.'
Pass – Grade B	'They will continue to need guidance to help them to develop and broaden their range of skills as teachers in post.'
Pass – Grade A	'They will benefit from further guidance in post but will be able to work independently'

One problem with this is that there is no means by which to ensure that teachers receive such guidance once in the workplace. UCLES have set up a 'tracking project' in order to see 'what happens to teachers in the first two years' after completing a CELTA course. It will look at what kind of jobs they have and how their career paths develop (University of Cambridge 2006). It is currently unclear however, how widely the results of this research will be disseminated.

Timmis (2000: 10) reports that he and colleagues at Leeds Metropolitan University (LMU) carried out a survey in the mid-1990s of ex-trainees once in post, and found that 70 per cent received 'no further structured professional development' in their first job. LMU felt that this suggested a need for a post-course development pack which would help novice teachers to examine their practices and to consider which of the techniques they had learnt were useful in their new context and to reflect on reasons for their abandonment of other techniques. This pack was intended to address the 'considerable anecdotal evidence of indiscriminate application of techniques, procedures and guidelines'.

A small scale piece of research was carried out by Dellar (1990) who looked at three novice teachers, who arrived in a private language school in Morocco. Two of the three novice teachers were fresh off a four week certificate course. She collected data from interviews with the teachers, observation of classes, and student feedback. Through the research, and in discussions with school managers, Dellar (1990: 63) identified a series of difficulties that the novice teachers faced, which she felt were due to 'a discrepancy between the content of IT [initial training], and what was ultimately expected of teachers in the school'. The issues were:

- 'problems of control';

- 'insufficient training' in certain areas, in particular dealing with monolingual classes and the issues that this raised in terms of the management of student use of the L1;

- 'inappropriate methodology', including over-emphasis on oral skills at the expense of reading and writing and 'inappropriate' use of pair and groupwork;

- difficulties in lesson planning, including poor understanding of timing, a lack of variety and a tendency to spend a large amount of time in preparation.

Dellar (1990) discussed the need to develop support for the new teachers, including a more in-depth induction programme, a initially lighter teaching load, a mentoring scheme with experienced teachers; weekly meetings and termly observation with the school director; recommendations of materials; and regular professional development workshops for all staff .

In a similar vein, Skinner (2002: 267) reflects on the experience of teachers who complete a CELTA course and embark on teaching abroad. Although not based on empirical research, the author makes some interesting points about the 'tension which exists between the culture of the training centre and the culture of the workplace'. She contrasts the 'collaborative collegiality' of the certificate programme with the isolation of the workplace or what Lortie (1975: 73) calls the 'private ordeal'. She writes of other difficulties that novices face, such as the contrasting values that they meet in the commercial language schools, the heavy teaching load, lack of opportunities for professional development and the sometimes negative attitudes of the more experienced, and sometimes entrenched, members of staff. Skinner recommends that initial training courses include a discussion of EFL careers, the use of case studies and more work aimed at helping novice teachers to self-assess their teaching (Skinner 2002).

Brandt (2006: 362) in a study of the teaching practice element of certificate courses felt that a view of 'teachers as contextually-isolated technicians' was a result of the emphasis of tutors on teaching practice as an assessment tool rather than as a means of developing the trainees' practice (seen as secondary). She felt that this view also led to too little attention being paid to the context in which the training was taking place. The tutors' focus on 'assessable performance' contrasted with the views of trainees who saw the primary role of the teaching practice as an opportunity to develop their skills as teachers.

Research methodology

The data reported here was part of a larger doctoral study which involved an exploration of a CELTA course carried out in a private language school in the UK. The course in its four week entirety was studied and data from multiple sources was collected: interviews with the trainees (beginning, middle and end of the course), observation of teaching practice and feedback, observation of all input sessions, a questionnaire (early in the course) and course-related documents including school publicity, handouts to trainees, and trainee-generated texts such as assignments and lesson plans. A follow-up questionnaire was also administered following the end of the course, whilst participants were in post.

This chapter reports on three of the participants from the study, Penny, Helen and Angela. The data which were used here are part of the total data set, and rely mostly on the interviews carried out with participants during the course and the post-course 'in post' questionnaire.

Findings

Penny

Penny embarked on a CELTA course because, assuming she passed the course, she was considering going abroad to teach. She also wanted to learn more about 'English and grammar', and she was keen to do 'something different' and mix with different people.

Many of Penny's key beliefs, expressed whilst on the CELTA, centred around affective factors in teaching and learning, for example the need to treat students as equals and to respect them as individuals.

> The relationship between teacher and student would not be successful if it wasn't a partnership [...] Everyone has a 'story' and a history. So learners bring something to a classroom. Learners who

Table 8.1

Teacher	Post-CELTA teaching	Data

Penny	Private language school, southern Europe. Teaching English to children.	• Course interviews
		• Questionnaire completed 4 months into first teaching contract
		
		• 2 emails:
		  – 6 months after starting job
		  – 9 months after starting job

Helen	Newly independent republic (former Soviet Union), working with students of nursing.	• Course interviews • Questionnaire completed 5 months into first teaching contract
Angela	Working as hourly contracted teacher for private language school in UK (same school as provided CELTA). Teaching adults and teenagers.	• Course interviews • Questionnaire completed 8 months into first teaching contract

resist will achieve very little – learners must be open to the known and the unknown.

Penny thought that students need a sensitive, encouraging teacher who uses humour and fun in the classroom both to create a relaxing environment and to involve students in the learning process. She expressed concerns that the teacher should not dominate the class or lecture students but should help individuals, working to keep their attention and build their confidence.

Penny felt that teachers needed to be knowledgeable about their subject, which she interpreted as English grammar and it was seen that over the duration of the course her understanding of grammar, which was initially very narrow, broadened, and she showed signs of reflection on the differences between L1 and L2 grammar needs and of the development of an understanding of pedagogic grammar. However, by the end of the course she still felt that her knowledge of grammar was inadequate and that developing this would lead to her being a better teacher.

In terms of learning to teach, Penny talked of the development of an individual style which did not involve mimicry of the more experienced teachers that she observed but developed with experience. She felt that learning from mistakes was an important aspect of learning. Despite this, indications were that she did not see herself as a teacher. She seemed reluctant even towards the end of the course to accept responsibility for her teaching, feeling that many of the problems she had faced in teaching practice related to the plan she had been given to follow or to the poor quality of the coursebooks she used. The following quotation about a well known ELT textbook illustrates this, 'lesson 14 showed that the textbook lacked the proper testing of the tasks, proofreading and editing necessary for the tasks to be carried out successfully'.

Following the end of the course, Penny took a job in a private language school in Southern Europe. Unlike the classes she encountered on the CELTA which consisted of multilingual adults from a range of cultural backgrounds living in the UK, Penny found that her students in her new context were quite different, monolingual classes of children. These students she felt were on the whole unmotivated and lacked interest in learning English, 'they do not pay attention and enthusiasm for English is low'. This led to problems with discipline.

She indicated that her planning had been reduced to preparation before teaching and that she felt this element of her CELTA preparation was not very realistic. Further, she stated that she had stopped using many of the teaching techniques taught on the CELTA, although she indicated that this was due to a difficulty with the culture of the country: 'to apply UCLES standards [here] is difficult. Many of the teaching methods laid down in the CELTA are more or less abandoned'.

Penny did not mention any support from colleagues that was available to her or other training post-qualification, with the exception of a British Council sponsored conference in the capital city. In fact, on returning to the UK at the end of a year, she described her job as 'traumatic', although she said that this was more to do with her relationship with the school owner than the teaching. She added that 'You have to do what the owners of the school say [...but...] screaming at the children in order to get classroom discipline is not my idea of fun (me not shouting causes a problem but unfortunately I'm not going to conform to their way of "teaching")'.

One of the difficulties facing Penny in her southern European teaching context seemed to be in the application of teaching techniques and skills to a context which differed considerably to that of the CELTA course. For Penny, differences were focused around the students' lack of awareness of the techniques she was using and to the pressure of teaching in a different school system in which 'the students do not know the CELTA teaching techniques and there's no time to explain'.

On the whole Penny was positive about the CELTA course, describing it as providing 'a good model' and a 'high standard of teaching'. The difficulty she faced in her teaching was ascribed to her national context and not to her CELTA preparation, 'In fact, the CELTA is not useful [here …]. If I were to continue teaching EFL and move to another country maybe the CELTA would be more useful [...] Teaching [here] may have been more of a shock and more difficult without it but I'm not sure.'

Despite her 'traumatic' experience, Penny seemed to want to remain in EFL although she had clearly rethought this as a long term prospect. Interestingly, even after a year of work, she did not see herself as a EFL teacher,

> Being here I've also discovered that teaching is not the career for me [...] My time [there] was traumatic [...] As a result I don't know whether to continue with TEFL. Of course, I'm not a teacher but if the circumstances were right TEFL-ing could prove useful for a while.

Helen

Prior to the CELTA course, Helen had left her profession as a midwife for the NHS and planned to teach English. She had previously worked as a midwife for a church group in Afghanistan.

In a similar vein to Penny, Helen was very concerned to avoid a teacher-dominated classroom. Whilst on the course she made frequent reference to the need to involve learners in the process of learning, to keep them active and to have 'student-centred', 'student-focused' teaching in which the teacher does not do all the talking but rather allows learners to speak. This major concern for Helen also included a belief that the teacher could learn from students, that the teacher didn't have all the answers, and a belief that the teacher should serve as a resource, along with students, for the classroom. Helen also spoke and wrote of the importance of adapting teaching to the learners' needs and styles of learning.

Another significant concern for Helen was the need to be sensitive and aware of learners and to make oneself available for them. She also mentioned a sense of humour and the need to keep lessons light-hearted in several places. Whilst variety was a key concern at the beginning of the course, by the end she realised that variety had to be consistent with lesson aims. Helen's clarity and systematic, well-organised approach to teaching was approvingly commented on over the duration of the course by trainers and fellow-trainees alike.

Helen was also clearly concerned with the related issues of feedback to students and dealing with errors in the classroom. In terms of language learning, Helen was concerned with communication and fluency, and a real world learning environment. And, in keeping with her concern with feedback, she spoke of the value of learning from mistakes. She spoke of her desire to have more feedback from course tutors, fellow trainees and also from learners of English as to her progress and effectiveness in the classroom.

Following the CELTA course, Helen took a job which involved teaching English to students of nursing in a newly independent republic of the former Soviet Union. In the questionnaire she indicated that she had not received any training in the country and that she did not have access to any professional journals or associations.

Helen contrasted the students she came into contact with on the CELTA with those in her job in terms of the multilingual groups of the CELTA versus the monolingual classes she found herself teaching. Now she had to learn to deal with the students 'switching to their own mother tongue so I have to be very strict about getting them to use English!'. She also noted the lower levels of English of her students. She did remark though that these differences had not really led to her changing her teaching approach.

She felt that her CELTA course had been a very useful and thorough preparation for her teaching, providing her with a variety of teaching techniques. She cited the teaching practice and subsequent feedback sessions as being 'especially helpful' and felt that the course could be usefully extended to give further teaching practice. Helen also felt that trainees on the course should be exposed to the different demands of teaching monolingual groups. As Penny had, Helen cited the less useful aspects of the course as being the 'in depth preparation' required on the course, noting that she now only uses 'a basic outline' in preparing for classes.

Angela

Angela began the CELTA course with no teaching experience but a range of other work experience such as bar and office work. Having travelled extensively, Angela was taking the course because she wanted to visit Australia and Asia following its completion, for a long period of travelling. She intended to teach in order to supplement these travels.

One of Angela's beliefs, expressed whilst on the course, related to the need for a teacher to be clear and to use examples when teaching in order to make teaching understandable for students. Angela talked about the need for a teacher to be organised and to plan carefully to achieve the aims of the lesson. She also mentioned the need to adapt teaching to suit the level and interests of the learners. Angela referred to adapting materials and the coursebook, again to the level of the students. She felt that this allowed the teacher to involve the students more in elicitation phases, hence increasing student involvement in the lesson, in addition to helping student understanding and working to build their confidence.

Angela was also clear in her belief in the need for teachers to be positive, energetic, enthusiastic and lively. She said that this helped to establish a good rapport between teacher and students, and hence increased student interest in the lessons. Student involvement was improved by giving students interesting tasks and games to play, and also by providing a challenge for them. Angela thought that it was important for the teacher to be confident, both with the subject and with the idea of experimenting with different methods of teaching. She felt that a confident teacher would make lessons more fun and would lead to the development of a comfortable and relaxed environment and hence to better rapport and increased levels of student interest.

Finally Angela spoke of the need to avoid the teacher dominating the classroom. She felt that students should be allowed and encouraged to speak, and student to student help could be useful in order to achieve this. She was clear that teachers should be patient with students and that teachers should treat them with respect and as equals. Angela was equally clear in her ideas about her own learning, 'you don't need to do anything with the good points', adding that you need to 'concentrate on negative points' and she followed this practice in her dealing with feedback from trainers and fellow-trainees.

Following the course Angela began working for the same school that had trained her which was a private language school in the South of England. In this job she was exposed to a wide range of different students and different kinds of teaching contexts. She was able, even in this first year of her teaching, to articulate the key issues and hence different approaches that she used for these different student groups. Some examples she gave were:

- Teaching refugees, some of whom have problems with literacy in their L1; requiring more visual aids and lots of revision.

- Teaching hotel staff, they were tired and unmotivated and often could not stay for the full lesson; focused on hotel-related vocabulary and phases.

- Teaching teenagers, with a low level of concentration; used more games and projects, used a quiz involving going around a town centre.

Although Angela indicated that she had not received any further training since completing the course, she did have access to a professional publication – *The EL Gazette*. She also had supportive colleagues who shared ideas with her.

Angela was clear about the useful elements of the CELTA course which she felt were learning how to plan to ensure variety, learning about different teaching methods, watching other people teach and practising herself. She felt that the assignments were of limited value and should be reduced, replaced with more models of teaching and planning, to include further observations of teaching in different settings and 'sample lesson plans given to students after they have taught lesson (to show how the teachers will do it)'. Angela also felt that she would have benefited from more input on grammar and how to teach different areas. Despite still being in her first year of teaching, Angela had a strong sense of the gaps in her knowledge post-CELTA and was able to identify and articulate areas where she felt that she needed help to develop as a professional teacher, for example she explained that she needed to improve her understanding of grammar and how to teach it.

Discussion

Although this is a case study of a small number of novice teachers, it has produced clear parallels with the conclusions of Dellar (1990) and Skinner (2002) who also highlighted the difficulties that novice EFL practitioners face in their first job. In this way case study methodology is able to build a mosaic of the disparate experiences of a group of people who are not always easy to access and whose experiences therefore have largely been unstudied.

It can be seen from the three cases that the participants all faced challenges in their first year of teaching. These challenges came in the main from the different contexts in which they found themselves teaching. Angela remained in the same context in which she had learned to teach although she found herself teaching a much wider range of students. She seemed to handle this well and was able to articulate her growing understanding of the influence of student need and context of teaching on approach. She was fortunate to have supportive colleagues with whom to exchange ideas and experience. The clarity and degree of detachment with which she was able to analyse the development of her practice on the CELTA, continued into her first year of teaching and allowed her to identify areas which needed to be improved.

In contrast to Angela, Penny and Helen took posts in unfamiliar teaching contexts, Penny working with children in a private language school in Europe and Helen teaching nursing students in a republic of the former Soviet Union. Helen, although recognising differences in her students and the classes essentially seemed to be able to adapt her teaching to her new monolingual, lower level teaching context. Possibly as a result of her previous experience of living a challenging environment, and despite the lack of support in her new post, she took these differences in her stride and was able to adapt her teaching to her new context.

Penny's experience in her first year of teaching English was strikingly different. Finding herself isolated and unsupported, teaching students for whom she had not been prepared to teach, she abandoned techniques that she had learnt on her CELTA and returned to the UK largely disillusioned. Despite her experience, she remained largely positive about her preparation for teaching, blaming her difficulties on the country in which she had taken a job.

Given the large number of people who qualify with certificates each year it is perhaps understandable and acceptable that there is attrition. Some people will leave because they only intended to teach for a few years before getting 'a proper job' and others will leave because they cannot find satisfaction in a job which has little career structure and where your experience and support is largely dependent upon the context in which you take a job. Penny's experience of training to teach adults and then being expected to unproblematically transfer that understanding and knowledge to the teaching of children is not uncommon in EFL. The lack of structured support however is difficult to accept.

Conclusion

Clearly, given the huge range of possible teaching contexts in which EFL practitioners can find themselves, the CELTA cannot prepare teachers for all eventualities. However, it is difficult to accept that trainees can be prepared for teaching in a context-independent way, using what are presented as culturally-neutral tools and techniques. Trainees need to reflect not simply on their developing expertise in using the tools and techniques of the profession but also must be helped to reflect and undertake dispassionate analysis of the use of those tools and techniques in culturally-situated practice. In this way, novice teachers will begin to develop a clear rationale and understanding of the development of their teaching approach, situated in the culture in which they work.

References

Brandt, C. (2006). Allowing for practice: a critical issue in TESOL teacher preparation. *ELT Journal,* 60, 355–64.

Dellar, G. (1990). The needs of novice teachers: A case study. In J. Roberts (ed.) *CALS Workpapers: Initial Training and the First Year in School* 1, 62–77. Reading: Centre for Applied Language Studies, University of Reading.

Ferguson, G. and Donno, S. (2003). One-month teacher training courses: time for a change? *ELT Journal,* 57: 26–33.

Gray, J. (2000). Training for reflective practice: getting the most out of pre-service courses. *The Teacher Trainer* 14, 14–17.

Haycraft, J. (1988). The first International House Preparatory Course – An historical overview. In T. Duff (ed.) *Explorations in Teacher Training: Problems and Issues* ,1–10. London: Longman.

Lewis, M. (2001). Straight talking: Qualifications and quality. *EL Gazette,* June, 257, 8.

Lortie, D. (1975). *Schoolteacher: A Sociological Study.* London: University of Chicago Press.

Phillips, D. (1989). *Pilot Study of the Career Paths of EFL Teachers.* London: Centre for British Teachers.

Roberts, J. (1998). *Language Teacher Education.* London: Arnold.

Skinner, B. (2002). Moving on: from training course to workplace. *ELT Journal* 56, 267–72.

Timmis, I. (2000). Sustaining development beyond pre-service training. *The IATEFL Teacher Trainers' SIG Newsletter* 1, 10–12.

University of Cambridge (2006). ESOL Exams: Certificate in English Language Teaching to Adults. Retrieved on 13th July 2006 from http://www.cambridgeesol.org/teaching/celta.htm

9 Ghosts on the cupboard: discursive hauntings during the first year of French Immersion teaching in Canada

Lace Marie Brogden and Becky Page

Introduction

In this chapter, we grapple with the interconnectedness of language, language teaching, and linguistic identities in pedagogical spaces. As noted in Farrell's introduction to this volume, although first year teacher induction studies are well represented in the literature (Howe 2006; Ingersoll and Smith 2004; McCann and Johannsessen 2004; Rogers and Babinski 2002), few studies detail the experiences of language teachers in their first year. Furthermore, in the context of literature pertaining to French Immersion settings, teacher induction is underrepresented. Teacher induction is 'the process of becoming a professional teacher … [and] includes acculturation through preservice, inservice, formal, informal and nonformal teacher education' (Howe 2006: 295). While other chapters in this volume address induction in the TESOL context, we provide examples from another language environment, specifically French Immersion in Canada, as a way of interrogating some of the 'hauntings', our metaphor for the discursive forces which appeared and reappeared in our work, and which we believe relevant to identity production of first year language teachers.

The purpose of our chapter is two-fold. On the one hand, there are stories to tell, and to query, our language/lessons as it were. On the other hand, we see interesting connections between the sometimes parallel, other times intertwined development of professional and linguistic identities – identities negotiated during pre-service teaching experiences that continue to be negotiated through the teacher induction process. These are the hauntings, the (im)possibilities, the (un)said.

While our examples are specific to French Immersion teaching, we believe our French Immersion context represents a one-off; that is, one which holds comparative possibilities for other language teacher (and teacher education) contexts.

We offer you, our reader, narrative fragments from our research project, presented here as a bricolage (Kincheloe 2005, 2001; Norma 2001) of tellings, inquiry and theory. Through this assembling, we include excerpts that reflect some of the ways our research data revealed certain interpellations – one might say callings or hauntings – of our teaching. One such example is this 'ghost' Becky talks about in her classroom:

> There is a counter along the back of my classroom. Sometimes when I'm teaching, I see her, sitting there, Professor X, from my university classes. And it's still a bit intimidating. I hear her talking curriculum, talking language, talking about how to teach. She doesn't say anything, but she's there. Instead of an angel on my shoulder, I've got a ghost on the cupboard. And she's a curricular ghost at that …

Our recollections help us question ongoing negotiations of French Immersion teacher identities during the induction year. Like Lieblich (2005), we

> often think that a lot of implicit analysis goes on in [the] editorial process, especially the sifting of the material into 'relevant' or 'interesting' on one hand, and 'irrelevant' or 'boring' on the other … scholars and readers alike should be aware of this process and try to reflect on its significance for each separate case. (p. 66)

We look to name, therefore, some of the discourses within which our often implicit negotiations may reside. Our attempt to name 'some of' these discourses is made in view of Apple's (1999) assertion that

> our social system is crisscrossed by axes of class, gender, race, age, nationality, region, politics, religion, and other dynamics of power. All of these produce differences, some of which are more strongly experienced than others depending on the situation. However, these sets of social differences are not isolated. They interact with each other in a complex nexus of power relations. (p. 3)

Consequently, our epistemological position is one located in view of both critical (Miller Marsh 2003; McLaren 1995) and poststructural (Butler 2004; Jackson 2001, 2004; St Pierre, 2000) paradigms. The multiple discourses at play in French Immersion teaching and learning are connected to other discourses not explicated in this chapter, nor even, in some cases, in our work thus far. While our textual strategies may at times seem fragmented or 'messy' (Denzin 1997), please know this is with intent. We realise such textual play carries a risk of leaving you, our reader, discouraged or unsatisfied, but invite you to dwell with us in a certain ambiguity – a space so often occupied by first year language teachers.

Background literature

French Immersion in Canada

French Immersion is a Canadian educational innovation (Rebuffot 1993; Lapkin *et al.* 1982) which provides French language instruction for non-French speaking students. The name is derived from the notion that students are 'immersed' in a French language environment at school. '[T]he distinguishing feature of immersion is that students learn language primarily through subject matter rather than by formal language teaching' (Day and Shapson 1996: 1). Depending on the model, this immersion begins in all subject areas as early as Kindergarten.

In the majority of French Immersion environments throughout Canada, the immersion teacher is positioned as the students' primary linguistic model (*Ministère de l'Éducation de la Saskatchewan* 1992). Beginning teachers negotiate this responsibility whilst constructing a professional identity during the first year of teaching and beyond. As noted at the beginning of this chapter, research addressing induction practices in French Immersion settings is scarce, and while studies of French immersion teacher identity and praxis are becoming more common (Brogden 2003; Sabo 2001; Laplante 1997; Day and Shapson 1996; Bernhardt 1992), they remain, overall, relatively unexplored in the literature.

In our querying of first-year language teacher experiences, we want to render explicit some of the paradoxes of our work. One such paradox is linguistic status. We work in language immersion contexts, contexts positioned as minority teaching environments. As such, we carry our (mostly) majority linguistic status, English, into our professional lives. Yet, in our professional roles, French becomes the language of privilege and we become part of the linguistic minority. It is within these contradictory environments of language and teaching and language teaching that we situate our stories.

The research context

The narrative fragments we share here were 'lived and told' (Clandinin and Connelly 2000: 20) over the course of the 2004–5 school year, and are recollected and retold in this writing. From 2004 to 2006, we worked together on a collaborative research between one university-based researcher and two teacher-researchers focused on the co-construction and ongoing negotiation of knowing and not knowing about first-year teaching in French Immersion contexts entitled *L'identité linguistique en tant que composante de l'identité professionnelle lors de l'insertion professionnelle: Deux enseignantes débutantes*[1] – Linguistic Identity as a Component of Professional Identity during the Induction Year: Two Beginning Teachers. While two teacher-researchers were involved in the year-long study, the focus of this chapter is on some if the experiences of one of the teacher-researchers, Becky Page, as well as on auto/ biographical reflections about those experiences by the university-based researcher Lace Marie Brogden.

During her first year of teaching, Becky taught at *École Monseigneur Blaise Morand*, an elementary (K-8) French Immersion centre in North Battleford, Saskatchewan, a community of 20,000 people, located 400 km North West of Regina on the banks of the North Saskatchewan River. The following excerpt reveals some of the tensions Becky says she perceived to be present in her work environment:

> While there is one Francophone school in our city, my school is the only immersion school in either the Public or Separate school divisions. This is important distinction to me because it means the only option for parents wishing to enroll their child in French Immersion in the greater community of North Battleford is École Monseigneur Blaise Morand, regardless of whether or not the family is of the Catholic faith. In my first year of teaching, I taught a Grade three class of 19 students.

Lace, the project's university-based researcher, teaches in the Baccalaureat Program at the University of Regina, a four-year, direct entry Bachelor of Education programme for pre-service teachers who intend to teach in French Immersion or French first language minority settings. Lace first worked with Becky in 2003, during Becky's third year of undergraduate studies. Following a 16-week internship semester, Becky and Lace once again worked together in a university setting in the winter of 2004, this time in the context of a course that encourages students to take a critical, informed position on teaching strategies in immersion contexts. The overarching goal of said course is that students complexify their own philosophy of teaching (in) French Immersion in Canada. The following excerpt, based on Lace's professional journal, helps illustrate her motivations for undertaking the project; she writes:

> In working together, Becky and I had the opportunity to begin a dialogue about some of the philosophical, pedagogical and political implications of language immersion teaching, a conversation that has continued as we pursue our research together. I keep returning to Pat Usher's (1996) work: one of the gifts of qualitative inquiry is the opening up of possibilities, possibilities for disrupting the structures that frame the way we 'do' schooling and the way we 'do' research. This study was no exception. Although I acted as principal investigator, and had initiated the study with the intent of better understanding first-year teacher experiences, I also came to new, altered understanding of my own teacher subjectivities. The telling and retelling of first year of teaching experiences have caused me to re:view tellings of my own teaching, and in the telling, have changed the way I teach, and the ways I come to (un)know.

Research methodology

Narrative knowing

Methodologically, our study privileged narrative inquiry; the narrative sense-making is a fluid process by which narrative schemas work to both organise and understand human experience (Bruner 2002, 1995, 1990; Clandinin and Connelly 2000; Turner 1996; Ricoeur 1991). As defined by Lieblich *et al.* (1998), narrative research can be 'any study that uses or analyzes narrative materials … it can be the object of the research or a means for the study of another question. It may be used for comparison … to learn about a social phenomenon … or to explore a personality' (pp. 2–3). Our research data took the form of narratives told and retold through tape-recorded conversations, journal reflections, and e-mail communications. In storying some of Becky's linguistic and professional identities during her induction year, and also some of Lace's negotiations of professional, researcher, mentor and becoming-colleague, we have engaged in sense making.

Event auto/biography

Auto/biographies, Nunan and Benson (2005) remind us, 'are a form of storytelling and stories are increasingly recognized as a legitimate way of knowing the world' (pp. 150–1). For our purposes, we used co-constructed event auto/biography, where the 'event' in question was that of the first year of language immersion teaching. Our research has been co-constructed in so much as we although we have assigned authorship to our narrative fragments, their tellings are collective, their meanings interconnected, their constructions interdependent. Event auto/biography captures moments in a life (Brogden, 2006), and there may be some grasp at knowing by examining said moments through research. In this grasp, we are, still and again, 'compelled to represent the auto/biographical moments of [our] research as partial, fragmented images of a story' (p. 913).

Findings

Hauntings

Over the course of our year long research project, we shared many cups of tea and many 'informal' conversations about the first year of immersion teaching, where 'informal is a synonym for serendipity' (Bernhardt and Schrier 1992: 115). Indeed, the metaphorical impetuous for this chapter, the 'Ghost on the cupboard' in Becky's classroom, emerged from the research data most serendipitously – one could even say it's 'appearance' was striking. Becky's comments about continuing to feel the presence – and pressure – of the expectations of her pre-service teacher development led us to numerous conversations about the usefulness (or not) of teacher education programming. An ongoing struggle was present in the difference between what Becky felt was expected of her and what she implemented in her classroom, as illustrated in her following comment:

> Recently, I had the opportunity to participate in a workshop, I have so much more subject area confidence now, I mean, it may not be perfect, but I think I can do some interesting things that will help my kids learn. She's still there though sometimes, Professor X,[2] watching me while I teach. And I still sometimes worry that perhaps I'm not doing it 'right'. Sometimes I wish I could just ask her a few more questions. My university classes were useful, but

> some things are just so much clearer to me now, I understand
> them differently.

The opportunity to maintain some connection to the university context by participating in the research project was identified as a positive outcome of our research project. Nevertheless, the theme of professional isolation, a trend we have identified in other teacher induction literature (see Baron (2006), for an example), was present throughout our research project, and was a theme experienced by teacher-researcher and university-based teacher educator alike.

Our research tells of negotiations of difference (what Benson (2005) calls diversity in the context of Second Language Acquisition literature); it describes spaces of uncertainty, conformity and growing professionalism. In so doing, it bumps into the discourse of normalisation (Popkewitz 1993 in Miller Marsh 2003), drawing on 'a variant of the discourse of difference [that] constructs members of nondominant cultures as being "different" from those who are members of the dominant culture' (p. 147). They reflect a pressure exerted on the part of the beginning language teacher to reenact perceived or imagined cultural norms; Becky comments:

> At the beginning of the year, I felt intimidated by some of my
> colleagues too. I'm not at all certain that this was deliberate on
> their part, but I felt uncertain just the same. Sometimes it was a
> comment in the staffroom, or at a meeting. Something said that
> would make me wonder if I knew enough French, or, perhaps,
> more accurately, the right French...

As evident in this description of Becky's honest, sometimes difficult and heartfelt reflections about negotiating her place in 'her' school, we observed the pressures of normalisation in the form of ongoing frustrations. In our observations, these frustrations were susceptible to being reinforced, rather than disrupted, by members of the educational community including colleagues, administrators, teacher educators, students and even ourselves.

Discussion

Although not specific to language teaching, we find resonance in Miller Marsh's (2003) work with two first-year teachers. In her work on *The Social Fashioning of Teacher Identities*, she observes 'what constitutes "normal" at Woodlawn [School] is a set of "appropriate behaviors" that have been sanctioned by the school' (p. 54). Like behaviours at Woodlawn, we argue the myriad discourses negotiated by language teachers happen in relation to other induction experiences *and* in relation to the ongoing negotiations of language itself.

Mentorship

Our work together speaks to us of the role mentorship can play in contributing to a positive induction experience. As Achinstein (2006) observes 'mentors' political literacy offers novices a way to act in the political climate of schools, to address inevitable conflicts with colleagues and administrators, and ultimately to move to define a professional identity' (p. 149). We see language as a critical, often politically charged aspect of the immersion teacher's linguistic identity, an identity which continues to develop and become more complex when s/he has access to generous, engaged language mentorship.

While we are, in the words of Chawla and Rawlins (2004), 'reluctant to offer any formula for co-constructing a mutually confirming and intellectually stimulating mentoring relationship' (p. 977), we hold to indications in our research that illustrate the possibilities for linguistic mentorship with beginning immersion teachers. As we believe to be the case for the students in our classrooms (be they the children in Becky's class or the university students in Lace's classes) our own linguistic identities continue to develop and become more complex when we have access to generous, engaged, language mentorship.

Early in our project, Becky's linguistic uncertainty and ambivalence surfaced frequently, as reflected in excerpts shared elsewhere in this chapter. But as the year progressed, Becky's linguistic confidence grew. The following reflection from late in Becky's first year of language teaching reflects some of the increasing complexities she brings to her teaching:

> I like my students and I like teaching. This year I have learned to stop being afraid of French. I think it is important for new teachers to find ways to speak French outside the walls of their classroom – to speak French with colleagues at school or in the community in order to talk with French speakers other than the students. I am more at ease with the language now, more comfortable, more confident really. I might make mistakes, but I will correct them, learn from them, and move on. Immersion teachers shouldn't be afraid – I am proud to speak French, and to speak in French.

We find Howe's (2006) work relevant once more. In concluding his international review of teacher induction practices, Howe notes 'the most successful teacher induction programs ... include opportunities for experts and neophytes to learn together in a supportive environment promoting time for collaboration, reflection and a gradual acculturation into the profession of teaching' (p. 295).

Related to the mentorship process, we also underscore the need for ongoing linguistic development of language immersion teachers in the induction year. We both work and teach in our non-dominant language; we are French language learners as well as French language teachers. In our study, two categories of ongoing linguistic development emerged. In the first instance, we believe beginning language immersion teachers continue – or *should* continue – to be language learners. As such, they will experience on-going learning related to grammar and vocabulary beyond their initial language and teacher training. One example of this evident in our work was '*le vocabulaire scolaire*' or school vocabulary, new curriculum-based terminology, 'kid' style, that was not always evident in our pre-service, second-language acquisition experiences. In the second instance, we draw attention to the impact of ongoing language acquisition on linguistic identity, such as the use of the target (or teaching) language outside classroom or school settings. For example, our project provided concrete opportunities for Becky to engage French interlocutors other than her school-based colleagues and students. Being involved in the presentation of our research at professional and academic conferences provided a rich layer of linguistic development and awareness in Becky's first year of teaching that may not have been present had she not engaged as a teacher-research in this project. Indeed, these opportunities to question and affirm her linguistic identity led Becky to see herself differently as a professional. Consequently, we encourage further study which examines the ongoing linguistic development of language teachers, particularly those working in minority language contexts such as French Immersion. Our research offers one example – that of engaging in teacher-research – of concrete ways in which beginning language teachers can develop their linguistic identities, and competencies, beyond their individual classroom context during the induction year; we are confident there are others.

Qualitative research is about opening up questions and generating possibilities (O'Reilly-Scanlon 2000), and our research is no exception. As expressed by Salomone (1992) in her case study work, our data 'must serve only as description, not as prescription' (p. 43). Through narrating the auto/biographical, we do not intended to provide answers so much as alternative ways of engaging curricular challenges. Consequently, the 'hauntings' we have shared here are intended to provide new spaces for the querying of language teacher education. We have done so with a view to invoking a certain resonance of the particular.

Conclusion

Like French Immersion, the interconnected environments of language classrooms and language teacher education classrooms are spaces where pre-service teachers and teacher educators alike risk finding themselves isolated, both linguistically and professionally. We believe this discourse of isolation also needs to be troubled. While it has been of import in our work, it is but one in collection of interconnected discourses at play in the first year of language teaching. Miller Marsh (2003) cautions that 'given the right conditions, any discourse can become authoritative … As teachers piece together fragments of discourse, they take on the ideologies inherent in them' (p. 150). Within the overarching theme of isolation presented here, the discursive pressures of the school staff room, curricular expectations, and performing to sociolinguistic norms are examples of the ideologies we found present during the induction year and have highlighted in this chapter. Many others merit further attention.

Amidst these discursive pressures, beginning language teachers, French Immersion teachers in our case, must negotiate their linguistic and professional identities in the continual becoming of and as a language teacher. Facilitating this process and supporting the induction process holds promise for our new colleagues, the students they will teach, and the profession as a whole. As Howe (2006) observes, 'the benefits of superior teacher induction include attracting better candidates, reducing attrition; improved job satisfaction; enhanced professional development and improved teaching and learning' (p. 287).

We conclude this chapter with an invitation for ongoing dialogue and reflection about new possibilities of and for teacher induction in language education settings. We believe an environment of reciprocal, collegial support and professional and linguistic mentorship can contribute to successful induction experiences for beginning French Immersion teachers, as well as to their ongoing linguistic development. We invite researchers, teacher educators, school-based administrators, mentor teachers and beginning teachers alike to open up such spaces for dialogue. Our hope is that the querying of our particular (French

Immersion) teacher stories holds possibilities for the negotiation of linguistic and professional identities by other beginning and mentor (language) teachers in the induction year and beyond. We leave the reader with final reflections, reflections we have written as individuals, but which stand as testimonies of what we see as the interconnected and continuously shifting character of teaching: Lace comments:

> In some ways, we are always becoming French Immersion teachers. Kumashiro's (2004) words echo. He maintains, in the context of anti-oppressive education, that we are always in the process of becoming, we never arrive, never master. This is a comforting discomforting notion to me. Grappling with issues of language teacher identity and induction lead to complexity, indeed. Through this research, I have learned to unlearn, learned to relearn. I am reminded as a researcher and a teacher of the importance of not knowing, of living the story that wants to be told. As Knowles and Cole (1994) observe, 'We're Just Like the Beginning Teachers We Study'. Indeed, perhaps I am just like the students I hope to teach – I am, linguistically and professionally, continually becoming, ever spiralling towards not-yet-knowable teaching destinations.

Becky comments:

> I'll get to teach Grade Three again next year, it's been decided. And parents are starting to request that their child be placed in my classroom. It's kind of a nice feeling. At the end of the day, there really is no ghost in the classroom, just me, and my students, and I know I can do a good job for them.

Notes

1. Authors' Note: This research project was made possible in part by a research grant from the French Education Research Fund of the Saskatchewan Instructional Development and Research Unit. The authors wish to thank Naomi Sara Fortier, research assistant for the project. Other findings from this study, as well as previous iterations of portions of this chapter, were presented in April of 2005 at CIRÉM (*Conférence internationale sur la recherche en éducation en milieu minoritaire de langue française*) in Ottawa, ON, at *Language Teacher Education*, a CARLA conference in Minneapolis, MN, June 2005, and at the AAAL/ACLA-CAAL conference in Montreal, June 2006.
2. Interestingly, during the collaborative writing of this chapter, Becky, having now completed her third year of teaching, noted that Professor X is no

longer 'there', commenting, '*She hasn't bugged me since; it was just my first year. Maybe I have her approval now*' (Field notes (LMB), 19 December 2006).

References

Achinstein, B. (2006). Mentors' organizational and political literacy in negotiating induction contexts. In B. Achinstein and S. Z. Athanases (Eds), *Mentors in the Making: Developing New Leaders for New Teachers* (pp. 136–50). New York: Teachers' College Press.

Apple, M. W. (1999). *Power, Meaning, and Identity: Essays in Critical Education Studies*. New York: Peter Lang.

Baron, W. (2006). Confronting the challenging working conditions of new teachers: What mentors and induction programs can do. In B. Achinstein and S. Z. Anthanases (Eds), *Mentors in the Making: Developing New Leaders for New Teachers* (pp. 125–35). New York: Teachers College Press.

Benson, P. (2005). (Auto)biography and learner diversity. In P. Benson and D. Nunan (Eds), *Learners' Stories: Difference and Diversity in Language Learning* (pp. 4–21). Cambridge, UK: Cambridge University Press.

Bernhardt, E. B. (Ed.). (1992). *Life in Language Immersion Classrooms*. Clevedon: Multilingual Matters.

Bernhardt, E. B. and Schrier, L. (1992). The development of immersion teachers. In E. B. Bernhardt (Ed.), *Life in Language Immersion Classrooms* (pp. 113–31). Clevedon: Multilingual Matters.

Brogden, L. M. (2003). L'actualisation linguistique en tant que composante de l'identité professionnelle chez les enseignant.es en formation. In J. Ardoino and G. Berger (Eds), *Former les enseignants et les éducateurs, une priorité pour l'enseignement supérieur: Actes du colloque*. Paris: Association Francophone Internationale de Recherche Scientifique en Education.

Brogden, L. M. (2006). Not quite acceptable: Rereading my father in *Qualitative Inquiry*. *Qualitative Inquiry,* 12 (5), 908–25.

Bruner, J. (1990). *Acts of Meaning*. Cambridge, MA: Harvard University Press.

Bruner, J. (1995). The autobiographical process. *Current Sociology,* 43 (2–3), 161–77.

Bruner, J. (2002). *Making Stories: Law, Literature, Life*. Cambridge, MA: Harvard University Press.

Butler, J. (2004). *Undoing Gender*. New York: Routledge.

Clandinin, J. and Connelly, M. (2000). *Narrative Inquiry: Experience and Story in Qualitative Research*. San Francisco: Jossey-Bass.

Chawla, D., and Rawlins, W. K. (2004). Enabling reflexivity in a mentoring relationship. *Qualitative Inquiry,* 10 (6), 963–78.

Day, E. M. and Shapson, S. M. (1996). *Studies in Immersion Education*. Clevedon: Multilingual Matters.

Denzin, N. (1997). *Interpretive Ethnography: Ethnographic Practices for the 21st Century*. Thousand Oaks, CA: Sage.

Gérin-Lajoie, D. (2003). *Parcours identitaires de jeunes francophones en milieu minoritaire*. Ottawa, ON: Prise de Parole.

Howe, E. R. (2006). Exemplary teacher induction: An international review. *Educational Philosophy and Theory, 38* (3), 287–97.

Ingersoll, R. M., and Smilth, T. M. (2004). Do teacher induction and mentoring matter? *National Association of Secondary School Principlas, NASSP Bulletin, 88* (638), 28–40.

Jackson, A. Y. (2001). Multiple Annies: Feminist poststructural theory and the making of a teacher. *Journal of Teacher Education, 52* (5), 386–97.

Jackson, A. Y. (2004). Performativity identified. *Qualitative Inquiry, 10* (5), 673–90.

Knowles, J. G. and Cole, A. L. (1994). We're just like the beginning teachers we study: Letters and reflections on our first year as beginning professors. *Curriculum Inquiry, 24* (1), 27–52.

Kincheloe, J. L. (2001). Describing the bricolage: Conceptualizing a new rigor in qualitative research. *Qualitative Inquiry, 17* (6), 679–92.

Kincheloe, J. L. (2005). On to the next level: Continuing the conceptualization of the bricolage. *Qualitative Inquiry, 11* (3), 323–50.

Kumashiro, K. K. (2004). *Against Common Sense: Teaching and Learning Toward Social Justice*. New York: RoutledgeFalmer.

Lapkin, S., Swain, M. and Argue, V. (1983). *French Immersion: The Trial Balloon that Flew*. Toronto, ON: The Ontario Institute for Studies in Education.

Laplante, B. (1997). Réfléchir à la langue en immersion. *Canadian Modern Language Review, 54,* 120–6.

Lieblich, A. (2005). Vicissitudes: A study, a book, a play: Lessons from the work of a narrative scholar. *Qualitative Inquiry, 12* (1), 60–80.

Lieblich, A., Tuval-Mashiach, R. and Zilber, T. (1998). *Narrative Research: Reading, Analysis and Interpretation*. Thousand Oaks, CA: Sage.

McCann, T. M., and Johannsessen, L. R. (2004). Why do new teachers cry? *The Clearing House, 77* (4), 138–45.

McLaren, P. (1995). *Critical Pedagogy and Predatory Culture: Oppositional Politics in a Postmodern Era*. London; New York: Routledge.

Miller Marsh, M. (2003). *The Social Fashioning of Teacher Identities*. New York: Peter Lang.

Ministère de l'Éducation de la Saskatchewan. (1992). *Français en immersion : Programme d'études pour le niveau élémentaire*. Regina, SK: Auteur.

Norman, R. (2001). *House of Mirrors: Performing Autobiograph(icall)y in Language/education*. New York: Peter Lang.

Nunan, D. and Benson, P. (2005). Conclusion. In P. Benson and D. Nunan (Eds), *Learners' Stories: Difference and Diversity in Language Learning* (pp. 150–6). Cambridge, UK: Cambridge University Press.

Popkewitz, T. S. (1993). *Changing Patterns of Power: Social Regulation and Teacher Education Reform*. New York: State University of New York Press.

O'Reilly-Scanlon, K. (2000). She's still on my mind: teachers' memories, memory-work and self-study. Unpublished PhD Thesis, McGill University, Montreal, Canada.

Rebuffot, J. (1993). *Le point sur... l'immersion au Canada*. Anjou, QC: Centre Éducatif et Culturel.

Ricoeur, P. (1991). *From Text to Action* (K. Blamey and J. B. Thompson, Trans.). Evanston, IL: Northwestern University Press (Original work published 1986).

Rogers, D. L. and Babinski, L. M. (Eds). (2002). *From Isolation to Conversation: Supporting New Teachers' Development*. Albany, NY: SUNY Press.

Sabo, J. E. (2001). The nature of teacher communication during mathematics instruction in two elementary French immersion classrooms. Unpublished master's thesis, University of Regina, Regina, Canada.

Salomone, A. M. (1992). Immersion teachers' pedagogical beliefs and practices: Results of a descriptive analysis. In E. B. Bernhardt (Ed.), *Life in Language Immersion Classrooms* (pp. 9–44). Clevedon: Multilingual Matters.

St Pierre, E. A. (2000). Poststructural feminism in education: An overview [Electronic version]. *Qualitative Studies in Education*, 13 (5), 477–515.

Turner, M. (1996). *The Literary Mind: The Origins of Thought and Language*. New York: Oxford University Press.

Usher, P. (1996). Feminist approaches to research. In D. Scott and R. Usher (Eds), *Understanding Educational Research* (pp. 120–42). London: Routledge.

10 From rats to language learners: the transition from the biochemistry laboratory to the language classroom in the first year of teaching

Y. L. Teresa Ting and Michael F. Watts

Introduction

If there is anything to be learnt from the metamorphosis of a biochemist into an EFL teacher, it is how comfort with research processes assisted professional transition. This chapter therefore does not detail how Teresa (ex-biochemist and novice EFL teacher) resolved teaching incidents, but recounts how two research-based tools enabled her to become an EFL professional despite 15-plus years as a positivistic scientist and an unsupportive professional context. This story inevitably goes beyond 'the first year' but presents praxis for preparing future teachers with tools to *survive and enjoy* not only *their* first years as EFL professionals, but many thereafter. Although teacher preparation now seeks to 'educate' rather than merely 'train' (e.g. Freeman and Richards 1993), ideal professional *tools* should nonetheless be easily learnable, *a priori*, through simple *training* if we want novice EFL teachers to develop a 'can do' professional identity before retirement lingers on the horizon. The two tools we describe here address the 'learnability criteria'. The first is actually a professionalised practice of positivistic scientist-training and is *the habitual reading of journal articles*, which empowered Teresa to access communal EFL/T knowledge despite an un-collegial environment. The second tool is *narrative inquiry* which Michael, in his role as academic mentor, introduced to Teresa. This co-authorship stories the metamorphosis of a hard-core scientist into enlightened EFL professional from both an internal and external perspective: trainee's and trainer's thoughts and voices intersect, and sometimes graphically, in a mutually constructed narrative to demonstrate how this small-scale teacher-friendly post-positivistic scholarship can transform teachers' reflections into insights for good practice.

As context shapes a novice teachers' professional outlook and construct of professional identity (see Beijaard *et al.* 2004), this story begins with a presentation of the *cult*-ure of Italian academia as a window onto the social and 'professional landscape' (Connelly and Clandinin 1999a) surrounding Teresa. The account of Teresa's professional transition is presented as a two-phase process. In the initial *'survival phase'* (see Maynard and Furlong 1995) Teresa buoyed herself through non-collegial torrents with the basic positivistic-research tool of regular journal article consumption. Survival gave way to *'professional development'* (*ibid*) as Teresa came to realise that numbers and statistics, the golden nuggets of the hard sciences, may be inadequate for guiding good EFL practice, prompting her to deconstruct her positivistic research identi-kit and incorporate notions of post-positivistic reasoning. An initially calm transition became more animated when Michael, as the MA-TEFL thesis adviser, handed Teresa the tool of *'narrative inquiry'*. As seen in some of the exchanges included here, tension was high as Teresa refuted the notion that EFL teaching and learning would benefit from a post-positivistic, qualitative approach. Ironically, in struggling to convince Michael of the beauty of numbers, Teresa came upon an emergent quantitative-qualitative difference which, in blending *narrative introspection* with *disciplined inquiry*, uncovered a possible explanation of why Teresa found classroom research less intimidating than colleagues hailing from the humanities. In closing, the reader is invited to consider the importance of instilling EFL teachers with a sense *membership in* the EFL community of practice since this would not only buoy novice teachers through their first years of classroom reality but, equipped with suitable research tools, may motivate teachers to investigate their practices and beliefs to eventually share their insights and thus contribute to the construction of the 'good-EFL-puzzle'.

Context

The nepotistic, baronistic ways of Italian academics have been discussed in *Nature* and *TIME* (Chu 2004): feudalistic thinking predominates Italian academia where who you know outweighs what you know. What is very revealing about the *Nature* articles is that they do not question the accusation that Italian academia favours compliancy and sycophancy over meritocracy but explains (away) the power-mongering practices as an inevitable outcome of a system that allows alliances to 'form along similar lines to those in the thirteenth century city states, [where] conspiracies and conspiracy theories abound' (Burr 1992: 273). Italy has opted for an academic *cult*-ure that 'has no incentive for high standards of science, and the appointment of the best scientists and scholars is not encouraged' (Aiuti 1992: 188). In fact, the best scholars, by international standards, were judged least 'scientifically mature' by committees whose criteria are not made public (Gaetani and Ferraris 1991) and despite legal actions, subsequently implemented measures nonetheless enable future committees to sidestep "the thornier issue of criteria for minimum qualifications – a fact that has not gone unnoticed by Italian academics' (Abbott 1995: 756). This non-attention to qualification is exactly how Teresa, with a PhD in neurobiology, became an EFL teacher in the Science Faculty at the local state University.

[Teresa continues the story ...] After several years, I realised that the Italian science community followed *cult*-ural norms too foreign for me to master, so, when presented the chance to become an EFL teacher, I accepted, becoming one of those 'individuals working abroad as EFL teachers, simply on the basis of being native speakers' (Ferguson and Donno 2003: 32). I actually entered during a 'closed' job-opening designed to re-hire the 30-plus local FL instructors when the Ministry of Education decided to re-hire FL-Lecturers under legally normalised contracts. Unfortunately for some, the Ministry also stipulated that candidates must have a university degree (not necessarily in FL teaching) recognised by the Italian Ministry of Education. Therefore, in the midst of an uproar, only a handful of the former FL teachers were re-hired, plus some new and very un-welcomed individuals – including me. To mollify this, a second round of hiring was undertaken whereby 'years of teaching experience' sufficed, allowing all former Lecturers to be re-hired but re-allocated where necessary. I thus became the intruder who had displaced one of four EFL instructors in the Science Faculty. Comments such as 'We much prefer our former colleague' and 'You teach when and where we tell you to' made it clear from the outset that collegial assistance was not on the agenda.

The situation was no brighter with the university students whose excuses for missing lessons reflected priorities quite different from mine: 'We made the annual supply of tomato sauce; it was my sister's birthday; my cousin got married.' Of approximately 10,000 students enrolling each year at the University of Calabria, more than 98 per cent are from the province of Calabria, reflecting how, despite the gloomy local unemployment figures lingering near 30 per cent, family proximity is important. Although Calabria has among the highest percentage of university graduates in Italy, it reflects two disturbing facts: (1) even if officially hired by local businesses, employees often sign monthly wage receipts of, for example €1,200, but receive only €600 and if unsatisfied, many are eager to accept; and (2) university tuition is low, based on family income, averaging €1,000/year.

Teaching English to unmotivated Italians and working with hostile foreigners was not my aspiration after 20 years of biomedical education and training. Lack of teacher-training was in itself a *complication* but, aggravated by the *setting*, my EFL teaching-emotion (Zembylas 2004) ran on 'empty'. I missed my laboratory rats.

Resolution: an old tool for survival and a new tool for development

Tool 1: Article consumption for accessing communal knowledge

In the absence of collegial support, I turned to the familiar professionalised positivistic tool of article-reading, devouring articles from academic as well as professional EFL/T journals to seek guidance from the international EFL community. In fact, my first task as a graduate student in neurobiology was to read a list of articles – not books. The importance of this will be discussed below. As scientific articles tend to reference other articles, I entered a self-regenerating unlimited information-gathering cycle and developed an understanding that positivistic knowledge is based upon small '*pieces of the puzzle*'. Moreover, members of the research team had taken turns to organise weekly seminars during which published articles were critically evaluated. This common praxis of positivistic researcher-training empowers aspiring scientists to understand that:

1. knowledge is public and accessible; *information gathering is feasible*

2. even the best publications must be scrutinised; *research becomes demystified*

3. published knowledge must be sound but not necessarily earth-shattering; research is *do-able* and *publishable.*

In retrospect, it was *this* understanding that articles provide updated professional insights plus the professionalised research-tool of article-consumption which gave me to access to the knowledge, practices and beliefs of my new EFL community, enabling me to at least *survive* the job of EFL instructor despite an inappropriate professional preparation. In addition to academic journals, I was pleased to find that the EFL community had *professional* journals where fellow EFL-teachers provided pragmatic ideas I could apply to my classrooms. I found myself before a critically-interactive EFL community which worked together to address a wide assortment of EFL issues: I had found helpful professional EFL practitioners.

Fuelled by expert ideas, I was soon transferring my positivistic research skills with cells *in vitro* on to EFL learners *in situ*. It was thus disheartening when my first submission to an academic EFL journal was rejected. Commenting on the graphs and statistics I had used to show that students in the 'experimental group', who had been given time to reflect on the contents of the lesson, obtained higher test scores than those of the 'control' group, the referee wrote: 'The numbers and percentages are not very informative on their own … A closer (qualitative) analysis of the individual reflections would … have been much more informative … what they actually wrote, how you analysed and "evaluated" them.' Rejection became 'epiphany' (Denzi 1989) as I realised that my purely quantitative ways were, by themselves, insufficient in the arena of EFL and, ignorant of what was meant by 'qualitative analysis', I was unable to share in community values and standards of conduct (Calderhead 1992, cf. Farrell 2003). I thus decided to pursue an MA-TEFL.

Tool 2: familiarity with small-scale qualitative research methods

Rather than a linguistic curriculum, I opted for an educational research programme, curious to understand how non-quantitative research could possibly accommodate the golden nuggets of positivistic Western science – *objective, reproducible* and *generalisable*. [… 'Ha!' … I thought to myself … 'Never!' …]

While I found the modules on EFL classroom practicalities and educational evaluation cognitively congruent, the module on action research was my first contact with post-positivistic reasoning which I found very challenging (although nowhere near as challenging as what was to come). It was, as I explained to my adviser, much like driving a

US-made car in the UK: 'I am dealing with many perceptual problems as my mind (car) is still hardwired to think quantitative; controlled vs. experimental, significant vs. non- and, most importantly, *repeatability* of findings.' However, by the end of the Action Research Module, I began to appreciate the place of action research in education, reflecting to my adviser that 'Action research attempts to comprehend human behaviour which is neither controllable nor amenable to manipulation. Positivistic control-vs.-experimental designs are thus unsuitable ... Action research does not seek *generalizable* prescriptive results but aims to sensitize those within the context to the context itself ... The principle beneficiary of classroom action research is actually the teacher, who, through the process of carrying out action research, is induced to think-out-loud and in depth, becoming a reflexive educator, gaining "practical wisdom" and "situational understanding".' Although I was still uncomfortable without numbers, I agreed with Stenhouse *et al.* (1985) that researching teachers are an invaluable source of field-based data for delineating not generalisable truths, but *transferable understanding* of learning/teaching processes.

The *need to research* prompted me to try my hand at action research after an advanced-level Italian professor commented: 'I can communicate but I can't express myself in English, as I can in French: I don't use native-like expressions.' Granted the goal of *native* has since been replaced by *communicative competence* (see Richards 2002), this eloquent Italian EFL-speaker nonetheless felt that native-like expressions would boost his English-id. I had not been trained to address such problems but by triangulating concepts from articles, exchanges with colleagues of other faculties and interviews with more advanced learners I began to define my own understanding of 'expression' and realised that authentic materials do not guarantee the generation of authentic expressions. Action research culminated in a pragmatic method for channelling learners' speech into more native-like utterances through children's L1-comics (Ting 2003).

Although 'non-academic', this was a milestone in my EFL-professional development. I had found a small piece of effective *transferable* classroom practice. Without numbers! EFL-*job* began to feel like EFL-*profession*. As acceptance of my first scientific article had inaugurated my science-professional identity, acceptance of my first EFL contribution gave me a sense of alignment with the broader teaching enterprise (Sim 2006): The '*teacher-socialization*' process (Blase 1986) had begun and feeling that I could indeed actively and successfully engage with the EFL community, 'me-biochemist' began giving way to 'me-EFL-teacher'.

As others before me, action research granted the novice a sense of 'professional' (Ginns *et al.* 2001).

My training in qualitative methods then moved yet farther from the safety of numbers when Michael entered the professional landscape as my final thesis adviser. As a life historian, he suggested that I undertake *narrative inquiry* to introspectively investigate what *I* understood about the place of quantitative-vs.-qualitative methods in educational research. I found Michael's suggestion that I study myself for my thesis quite challenging ['… and about as academic as the daily horoscope …'] as how can one person's professional story be useful for others? ['… and who in their right minds would want to read it? …']

Significantly, not only had Michael taught innovative EFL when he had been working overseas in Cambodia (Watts 1994a; 1994b) but he had also had reservations about qualitative research (Watts 2007). So he was, in Lave and Wenger's terms (1991), a young master or journeyman in the community of qualitative educational researchers. This meant that I had found someone to identify with as I attempted to understand the qualitative nature of the EFL community. However, this identification took time.

Disciplined inquiry

In encouraging EFL teachers to undertake research, Borg (2003) suggests that 'disciplined inquiry' may be a means to integrate quantitative objective hypothesis-testing into detailed narratives of learning/teaching processes, as qualitative information is what most teachers would prefer to rely on to re-evaluate their practices. This section describes such a disciplined inquiry: while weaving her life-history narrative through her educational, social and professional fabric, Teresa came upon some emergent and unexpected findings, investigated their implications and came to understand why some EFL colleagues may find classroom-research so foreboding. This prompted Teresa to consider how praxes of biochemist-training may be transposed on to EFL-teacher education to cultivate EFL teacher-researchers and is an example of how a non-numerical narrative approach – the very practice she had hoped to discredit – actually supported Teresa's full professional metamorphosis into an enlightened EFL practitioner.

While she had gained some respect for action research, Teresa found narrative inquiry 'too woolly for comfort' and set about persuading Michael of the power of numbers, presenting him histograms and graphs showing how coffee caused baldness, which *if* true, would surely have convinced him never to drink coffee again. Surprisingly, Michael was not swayed by Teresa's quantitative tactics: 'I'm not saying there's anything wrong with these numbers, Teresa. But I'd sooner give up my hair than my coffee. You are assuming (I presume) that men don't want to be bald – or, at least, that they are prepared to give up coffee to, if I can put it this way, keep their hair on. And so I would argue that these numbers speak in a limited way.'

This lack of excitement with numbers re-echoed the criticism of the journal referee, leading Teresa to suspect that the 'piece-of-the-puzzle' approach of positivistic research may not be how educators tackle problems. Just how 'they' did it remained a mystery until Teresa made an off-the-cuff statement regarding her reading: 'Reading two books is mind-settling while reading 40 articles is mind-opening.' When Michael responded that articles could be highly redundant and not mind-opening at all, Teresa's suspicion was transformed into *emergent understanding*: 'Maybe educators expect more than a mere piece-of-the-puzzle from single research endeavours? Maybe they expect something much bigger – *a masterpiece*, so to speak.'

To test her hypothesis that qualitative and quantitative scholars sought dimensionally different research-findings, Teresa conducted a simple quantitative investigation on the citation profiles of positivistic and post-positivistic scholars, counting the books and journal articles that the authors of two education textbooks on narrative inquiry and two scientific neurobiology textbooks cited. The post-positivistic scholars cited books over journal articles at a ratio of 4:1 while positivistic peers favoured articles over books at a ratio of 9:1 (Ting 2005a). This simple investigation, although limited, allowed Teresa to confirm her hypothesis that scientists contextualise themselves amongst *pieces of the puzzle* (articles) while educators appear to prefer '*bigger pictures – masterpieces*' (books) to back their assertions, even if they do publish academic journal articles.

More important than the implications for teacher-training (discussed below), this was an important moment in Teresa's professional development as this knowledge had not been gained through the positivistic process of *a priori hypothesis testing* but through the *recognition of emergent patterns,* a qualitative research process: without the blinders of a positivistic research design, Teresa perceived the emergent. And what of qualitative research criteria? Teresa was not surprised by scientists' preference for articles, reflecting to Michael that positivism cultivates what Stake (1978) calls single-issue researchers who share a generalisable truth which can 'transcend opinion and personal bias' (Denzin and Lincoln 1998: 7). Pieces of the puzzle must fit. As some findings occasionally impose a reshaping of space in this common puzzle, *objective* becomes an essential criteria of positivistic research. Consequently, positivism favours a *piece-of-the-puzzle* approach as small impositions are easier to accept and *reproducibility* easier to guarantee with smaller dimensions … What troubles me is how qualitative research can achieve the criteria of *objective* and *reproducible?* Clearly it cannot. Therefore, what criteria *validate* post-positivistic research?' By way of response, Michael suggested that Teresa was still trying to fit a round quantitative peg into a square qualitative hole, struggling with the essential differences between qualitative and quantitative research and positivist and post-positivist frames of reference: She was, in her words, 'cemented by the hegemony of numbers onto the positivistic end of the research spectrum'.

What began to shift her understanding was the concept of 'idiosyncratic' which Teresa encountered through a compilation of action research case studies whereby 66 EFL practitioners across the world shared how action research was adopted to delineate solutions to a variety of EFL classroom problems (Richards 1998). After diving into and emerging from the vast number of storied cases covering a global array of learner demographics and teaching situations, Teresa realised that classroom research must accommodate *idiosyncrasy:* 'While the development of biodegradable plastics or cancer-fighting drugs is valid regardless of context, "education" is highly contextual and defies the testing of hypotheses formulated *a priori*. This does not imply that education is not *researchable*. On the contrary, educational research requires a more agile yet rigorous practitioner who, even in the absence of numbers and statistics is able to tightly argue their research process, data interpretation and results to *inform* and *sensitise* us to clues we might otherwise have missed (Eisner 1991; Denzin and Lincoln 1998). In seeking transferable understanding and knowledge that informs practice, postpositive methods rely on dense descriptions which allow readers to access the context, evaluate whether researcher interpretation is believable and subsequently *transfer* the *understanding* obtained from one idiosyncratic context onto another' (Lincoln and Guba 1985).

In weaving her life-history narrative through this small patch of data obtained from disciplined inquiry, Teresa came to understand why positivistic and post-positivistic scholars tended to position their works among *dimensionally different* chunks of information: 'Given the idiosyncratic nature of classrooms, post-positivistic methods offers educational research a means to access and better understand the complexities of learning and teaching ... and with the added element of "culture" (Alptekin 2002) in EFL classrooms, EFL learners cannot be – alas! – "experimented on" like rats.' Teresa now understood why Michael and the journal referees were not charmed with barren numbers.

In addition, enlightened to the notion of 'emergent understanding', Teresa began to see how these findings may explain why she found classroom research less intimidating than colleagues hailing from the humanities: Trained on articles, scientists feel comfortable contributing small *pieces of the puzzle* to their communities of practice, while teachers, if trained primarily on books (see Pendry and Husbands 2000), may come to believe that valid contributions must provide '*book-sized masterpiece insights*'. This would hinder teachers from disseminating their smaller-scaled classroom-based research findings, depriving the EFL community of invaluable field-based understandings of (in)effective classroom practices. This concern prompted Teresa to suggest a praxis regarding EFL teacher-researcher education (Ting 2005a), and recognising the importance of *narrative inquiry* as a teacher-friendly medium for transforming tacit teacher knowledge into communal understanding, Teresa encouraged EFL colleagues to narrate the difficulties and successes of teaching science in content-based EFL initiatives. The very challenging arena of content-based EFL teaching was enriched by the 'Voices from the CLIL classroom' (Ting *et al.*, 2006) and Teresa finally engaged with the EFL community.

Engaging with the EFL community of practice

Our professional sense of belonging increases through processes of engagement and alignment with those sharing a common enterprise in what Lave and Wenger (1991) term a 'community of practice'. Their work on situated learning rejects the notion of learning as a social knowledge transfer in favour of learning by 'doing' and 'being', leading, therefore, to the formation of a *professional identity*. Be it apprentice tailors (Lave and Wenger 1991) or physicists (Wenger 2000) or educational researchers (Hodkinson 2004) the concern is not with tailoring or physics or educational research but with *being* a tailor or physicist or educational researcher. Likewise the construction of language teachers' professional identity (Singh and Richards 2006). Wenger identifies three key elements underlying communities of practice: mutual engagement; joint enterprise; and a shared repertoire which is 'created over time by the sustained pursuit of a shared enterprise' (Wenger 1998: 45). Whilst this may suggest the need for physical proximity, communities of practice can be held together at a distance by other forms of communication (Wenger 2000; Hodkinson 2004). In fact, in the absence of collegial support, Teresa engaged with her newfound community of practice through journal articles which initially enabled her to share in communal repertoire and subsequently guided her contributions to the joint enterprise of defining 'good EFL practices'. It was the understanding that: (1) the EFL community extends far beyond the reaches of the Science Faculty where she teaches; and (2) communal knowledge is built upon small contributions from individual members, which motivated Teresa to seek ways of researching her EFL-classroom practices.

This invaluable *research attitude*, instilled upon her during her biochemist-training, buoyed Teresa through her *survival stage* as an EFL-teacher. Ironically, it was the rejection of her statistical ELT article that obliged Teresa to re-evaluate her already uncomfortable position on the periphery of this community, prompting her towards *professional development*. It was actually the very non-numerical qualitative tool of narrative research which enabled Teresa to deconstruct her positivistic beliefs, giving her the means to appreciate both the strengths and the limitations of her professional identity as biomedical researcher within her new context of EFL practitioner. Despite her earlier reluctance to consider it a valid and valuable source of data, rigorous inquiry into her own life as biochemist and then as EFL teacher enlightened her to the importance of post-positivistic research in education. Thereafter, she became better assimilated into the EFL community of practice which welcomed her qualitative small-scale contributions. In fact, although she, as many classroom teachers, continually develop classroom tools, it was the process of investigating her own life history that encouraged her to recognise reflective and reflexive classroom practices as valid forms of research through which invaluable transferable insights can be gained. These are, after all, small pieces of the bigger 'good-EFL-education' puzzle.

The final part of her transition from 'me-biochemist' to 'me-EFL-teacher' occurred during the year it took her to complete her MA thesis (Ting 2005b). It should be remembered that to participate in this particular community of practice, Teresa had needed to negotiate quantitative barriers erected over 15 years in the biochemistry lab. Others may well find that their routes to such participation are littered with fewer obstacles. Nonetheless, a year may still be too long for TEFL certificate courses. However, whilst certificates may signpost the community of professional EFL teachers, full participation in that community requires more than this: it requires that the participant, and the wider community, recognise participants' place through their contribution as professional membership is about cultivating a sense of *belonging*. And such as sense of belonging motivates us to (re)search means for improving communal practices (Cochran-Smith and Lytle 1999).

While good research and good teaching are not necessarily indicative of each other, some (and probably many) EFL teachers may be potentially insightful practitioner researchers. Would the EFL community not benefit greatly, therefore, if teachers, as biochemists, are cultured into this *participant research attitude* and feel the need to contribute to the 'good-EFL-practice puzzle' by investigating and sharing their classroom-based experiences, should they wish? However, to develop a positive attitude towards research, teachers must become users of the research literature (Haley and Rentz 2002; Counsell *et al.* 2000; Shkedi 1998) and feel comfortable with the research act itself (Borg 2006). More importantly, as researching is not the *raison d'être* of teachers, if we wish to encourage busy teachers to undertake research, they must be equipped with teacher-friendly small-scale post-positivistic research tools such as action research, case-studies and reflective narrative inquiry. In encouraging reflective-teaching, Schön foresaw the potential of these new scholarships as 'What else could they be? They will not consist in laboratory experimentation or statistical analysis of variance' (1995: 31; cf. Evans *et al.* 2000: 406). To extend Dewey's democracy of education to the education of teacher-researchers who can contribute to the good-EFL-puzzle, the research process must be demystified. To attain an educational agenda enriched with teachers' voices, teacher-education should consider adopting the practices of biochemist-training whereby the regular reading and critiquing of published articles *demystifies research* empowering trainees with the knowledge that *information is accessible, research is doable* and *information dissemination possible* (Ting 2005a). Only if teachers see themselves as part of the knowledge-generating process will they transform the tacit knowledge bound in personal journals entries into journal articles, publishing and thus rendering their insights accessible to their community of practice (Somekh 1993; Burton 2005; Cochran-Smith and Lytle 1999). More importantly, in engaging in small-scale qualitative research, teachers themselves will give shape to the much needed definition regarding the discourse, utility and texture of such teacher-friendly scholarships which have been criticised, interestingly, for not meeting positivistic standards (see

Hargreaves 1996; Prain 1997; Evans and Benefield 2001; Bullough and Pinnegar 2001; Hammersley 2000).

Implemented in a teacher-education programme, narrative inquiry offers novice teachers a tool for overcoming those personal beliefs which may form professional obstacles (Farrell 2003). It was, in fact, in rendering 'implicit beliefs explicit' (Uhlenbeck *et al.* 2002: 249) through the language of narration that Teresa uncovered the 'contradictory beliefs underlying [her] practice' (*ibid*): the *reproducibility criteria* she used to qualify biomedical research was impertinent to investigating EFL-learning/teaching processes as these are not mere 'knowledge-transfer events' (e.g. Smith 2001). The narrative is invaluable for storying changes in teachers' beliefs (Connelly and Clandinin 1999b), the foundations upon which practice is grounded and, if shared, would give us access to the 'tacit professional knowledge' (Freeman 2002) dispersed throughout our community of practice. 'In seeking to understand more about the processes involved in learning to teach we have come to recognise the strength of the personal agendas that beginning teachers bring with them and the active role they play in negotiating their own learning' (Hagger and McIntyre 2000: 483). Narrative inquiry takes emancipatory teacher-reflection (Farrell 1999a; 1999b) a step forward as it offers a medium to render such inner processes 'conscious' and, laid upon a 'story structure framework' (Farrell 2006), could become sufficiently tangible to inform teacher-education.

In addition, familiarity with the narrative also sensitises us to the idiosyncratic nature of learning/teaching since classrooms are containers of variegated social, cultural and very individual (hi)stories. James Alatis, the 'father of TESOL' defined 'the best teacher' as one who '[cherishes] their students and holds them in unconditional positive respect' (Ancker 2004: 7). In addition, good EFL teachers have the added responsibility of 'knowing something about the students' language' (*ibid*, p. 5) and be enlightened to the culture behind the learner'. For EFL teachers who are often foreign to the cultures of their learners, narrative inquiry becomes an invaluable tool for overcoming prejudices which stop us short of cherishing our learners and their ways of being. It is a tool with which we can modulate our beliefs and thus our practices (Golombek 1998; Richards *et al.* 2001), providing benefits beyond professional development as it settles us into our contexts and render us more comfortable with the perspective of others. Through the narrative lens, Teresa now appreciates the other side of the coin: behind the non-meritocratic *cult*-ure lies an established and highly interwoven society whereby everyone is somehow related to everyone else. The up side of such a tightly-knit culture is that it sustains *all* individuals, materially, monetarily, and even professionally and thus, personally. Despite high unemployment, everyone has a roof, food and even a cellphone and someone to call, as well as time to *live*: tomato sauce and cousins' weddings are prioritized over English lessons.

Conclusion

This co-narrated story has highlighted moments within the professional transition of a number-locked biochemist into an enlightened EFL practitioner, and documented the two tools which enabled Teresa to surpass external complications presented by the local professional landscape and resolve internal complications arising from the fossilised understanding that research, to be called such, must produce quantifiable and generalisable truths through reproducible methods and samples. Cultivating trainees to regularly access and critique published research articles based on action research and narrative inquiry carried out by EFL teachers would merge the two tools that enabled Teresa to bridge the abyssal gap between the biochemistry laboratory and the EFL language laboratory: article reading gave Teresa access to updated knowledge and familiarity with relevant themes and discourse while narrative inquiry empowered her to become a more reflective and reflexive EFL practitioner, better positioned to engage with an educational community of practice. This case study has therefore reported not so much Teresa's EFL teaching but how she came to identify herself, and be identified as, an EFL teacher. Two decades ago, Richards (1987) suggested that effective TESOL teacher education must, among others, develop principles by which the language teachers are prepared. Although various EFL approaches have come and gone, his goal for TESOL teacher preparation remains irrefutable: 'The student teacher must adopt the role of autonomous learner and researcher ... the role of the teacher educator ... [is to] guide the student teacher in the process of generating and testing hypotheses and in using knowledge so acquired as a basis for further development' (*ibid*, p. 223). The cultivation of a research attitude complimented by teacher-friendly reflective research tools for supporting reflexive practice may not only attenuate the 'reality shock' (Veenman, 1984) of first-year classroom teaching but, more importantly, sustain lifelong professional development by instilling teachers with a sense of 'participation' in the thriving global EFL community, regardless of local professional landscapes.

References

Abbott, A. (1995). Concorsi 'corruption' leads to court. *Nature, 374,* 756.

Aiuti, F. (1992). Italian promotions defended and attacked. *Nature, 356,* 188.

Alptekin, C. (2002). Towards intercultural communicative competence in ELT. *English Language Teaching Journal,* 56 (1), 57-64.

Ancker, W.P. (2004). The psychic rewards of teaching: an interview with James E. Alatis. *English Teaching Forum,* 42 (2), 2–8.

Beijaard, D., Meijer, P. C. and Verloop, N. (2004). Reconsidering research on teachers' professional identity. *Teaching and Teacher Education,* 20, 107–28.

Blase, J. J. (1986). Socialization as humanization: one side of becoming a teacher. *Sociology of Education,* 59, 100–13.

Borg, S. (2003). Research in the lives of TESOL professionals. *TESOL Matters,* 13 (1), 1–5.

Borg, S. (2006). Research engagement in English language teaching. *Teaching and Teacher Education,* 23, 731–47. Bullough, R. V. and Pinnegar, S. (2001). Guidelines for quality in autobiographical forms of self-study. *Educational Researcher,* 30, 13–22. Burr, D. (1992). Italian university structure. *Nature,* 357, 273.

Burton, J. (2005). The importance of teachers writing on TESOL. *TESL-EJ,* 9 (2), 1–18.

Calderhead, J. (1992). Induction: A research perspective on the professional growth of the newly qualified teacher. In: J. Calderhead, and J. Lambert, (eds), *The Induction of Newly Appointed Teachers,* (pp. 5–21). General Teaching Council, London.

Chu, J. (2004). How to plug Europe's brain drain. *TIME,* 19 January, 32–39.

Cochran-Smith, M. and Lytle, S. (1999). The teacher research movement: a decade later. *Educational Researcher,* 28 (7), 15–25.

Connelly F. M. and Clandinin, D. J. (1999a). *Shaping a Professional Identity: Stories of Education Practice.* London, ON: Althouse Press.

Connelly F. M. and Clandinin, D. J. (1999b). Stories of experience and narrative inquiry. *Educational Researcher,* 19 (5), 2–14.

Counsell, C., Evans, M., McIntyre, D. and Raffan, J. (2000). The usefulness of educational research for trainee teachers' learning. *Oxford Review of Education,* 26 (3-4), 467–82.

Denzin, N. (1989). *The Research Act.* Englewood Cliffs, NJ: Prentice Hall.

Denzin, N. K. and Lincoln, Y. S. (1998). *Strategies of Qualitative Inquiry.* London: Sage.

Eisner, E. W. (1991). *The Enlightened Eye: Qualitative Inquiry and the Enhancement of Educational Practice.* New York, NY: Macmillan.

Evans J. and Benefield, P. (2001). Systematic reviews of educational research: does the medical model fit? *British Educational Research Journal,* 27 (5), 527–41.

Evans, M., Lomax, P. and Morgan, H. (2000). Closing the circle: action research partnerships towards better learning and teaching in schools. *Cambridge Journal of Education*, 30 (3), 405–19.

Farrell, T. S. C. (1999a). Reflective practice in an EFL teacher development group. *System*, 27, 157–72.

Farrell, T. S. C. (1999b). Teachers talking about teaching: creating conditions for reflection. *TESL-EJ*, 4 (2), 1–13.

Farrell, T. S. C. (2003). Learning to teach English language during the first year: personal influences and challenges. *Teaching and Teacher Education*, 19, 95–111.

Farrell, T. S. C. (2006). The first year of language teaching: imposing order. *System*, 34, 211–21.

Ferguson, G. and Donno, S. (2003). One-month teacher training courses: time for a change? *English Language Teaching Journal*, 57 (1), 26–33.

Freeman, D. (2002). The hidden side of the work: Teacher knowledge and learning to teach. *Language Teaching*, 35, 1–13.

Freeman, D. and Richards, J. C. (1993). Conceptions of teaching and the education of second language teachers. *TESOL Quarterly*, 27, 27–45.

Gaetani, G. F. and Ferraris, A. M. (1991). Academic promotion in Italy. *Nature*, 353, 10.

Ginns, I., Heirdsfield, A., Atweh B. and Watters, J. J. (2001). Beginning teachers becoming professionals through action research. *Educational Action Research*, 9 (1), 111–33.

Golombek, P. R. (1998). A study of language teachers' personal practical knowledge. *TESOL Quarterly*, 32 (3), 447–64.

Hagger, H. and McIntyre, D. (2000). What can research tell us about teacher education? *Oxford Review of Education*, 26 (3–4), 483–93.

Haley M. H. and Rentz, P. (2002). Applying SLA research and theory to practice: what can teachers do? *TESL-EJ*, 5 (4), 1–7.

Hammersley, M. (2000). The relevance of qualitative research. *Oxford Review of Education*, 26, 393–405.

Hargreaves, D. (1996). *Teaching as a Research Based Profession: Possibilities and Prospects*. London: London Teacher Training Agency.

Hodkinson, P. (2004). Research as a form of work: expertise, community and methodological objectivity. *British Educational Research Journal*, 30 (1), 9–26.

Lave, J. and Wenger, E. (1991). *Situated Learning: Legitimate Peripheral Participation*. Cambridge: Cambridge University Press.

Lincoln, Y. S. and Guba, E. G. (1985). *Naturalistic Inquiry*. Beverly Hills, CA: Sage.

Maynard, T. and Furlong, J. (1995). Learning to teach and the models of mentoring, in: T. Kerry and A. S. Mayes (eds), *Issues in Mentoring* (pp. 10–24). London: Routledge.

Pendry, A and Husbands C. (2000). Research and practice in history teacher education. *Cambridge Journal of Education*, 30, 321–34.

Prain, V. (1997). Textualizing your self in research: some current challenges. *Journal Curriculum Studies*, 29 (1), 71–85.

Richards, J. C. (1987). The dilemma of teacher education in TESOL. *TESOL Quarterly*, 21 (2), 209–26.

Richards, J. C. (1998). *Teaching in Action: Case Studies from Second Language Classrooms*. Alexandria VA: TESOL.

Richards, J. C. (2002). 30 Years of TEFL/TESOL: A personal reflection. *RELC Journal*, 33 (2), 1–35.

Richards, J. C., Gallo, P. B. and Renandya, W. A. (2001). Exploring teachers' beliefs and the processes of change. *PAC*, 1 (1), 41–62.

Schön, D. A. (1995). The new scholarship requires a new epistemology, *Change*, November/December, 27–34.

Shkedi, A. (1998). Teachers' attitudes towards research: a challenge for qualitative researchers. *Qualitative Studies in Education*, 11 (4), 559–77.

Sim, C. (2006). Preparing for professional experiences – incorporating pre-service teachers as 'communities of practice'. *Teaching and Teacher Education*, 22, 77–83.

Singh, G. and Richards, J. C. (2006). Teaching and learning in the language teacher education course room: a critical sociocultural perspective. *RELC Journal*, 37 (2), 149–75.

Smith, J. (2001). Modeling the social construction of knowledge in ELT teacher education. *English Language Teaching Journal*, 55 (3), 221–7.

Somekh, B. (1993). Quality in educational research – the contribution of classroom teachers. In: J. Edge and K. Richards (eds), *Teachers Develop Teachers Research* (pp. 26–38). Oxford: Heinemann.

Stake, R. E. (1978). The case study method in social inquiry. *Educational Researcher*, 7 (2), 5–8.

Stenhouse, L., Rudduck, J. and Hopkins, D. (1985). *Research as a Basis for Teaching: Readings From the Work of Lawrence Stenhouse*. Portsmouth, NH: Heinemann.

Ting, Y. L. T. (2003). Real conversational English: children's comics for advanced adults. *Modern English Teacher*, July, 41–3.

Ting, Y. L. T. (2005a). Empowering the teacher-researcher: adopting a tool from biochemist-researcher training. *TESL-EJ*, 9 (2), 1–13.

Ting, Y. L. T. (2005b). *The Value of Narrative Inquiry in Professional Development: A Case Study in Recognising the Value of Equilibrated Qualitative and Quantitative Methodologies in Teacher-Led Classroom Research*. Cosenza: Università della Calabria.

Ting, Y. L. T., Micelli, C., Newell, J., Parise, G. and Rossi, R. (2006). Voices from the CLIL-classroom: what do subject teachers, language teachers and students have to say about what makes for successful CLIL. *XXXI TESOL-Italy Conference*, 3–4 November.

Uhlenbeck, A. M., Verloop, N. and Beijaard, D. (2002). *Teachers College Record*, 104 (2), 242–72.

Veenman, S. (1984). Perceived problems of beginning teachers. *Review of Educational Research*, 54 (2), 143–78.

Watts, M. (1994a). *Speaking English in Cambodia*. Phnom Penh: University of Phnom Penh.

Watts, M. (1994b). *Eleven Plays for Cambodian Students of English*. Phnom Penh: University of Phnom Penh.

Watts, M. (2007). They have tied me to a Stake: reflections on the art of case study research. *Qualitative Inquiry*, 13 (2), 204–17.

Wenger, E. (1998). *Communities of Practice: Learning, Meaning, and Identity*. Cambridge: Cambridge University Press.

Wenger, E. (2000). Communities of practice and social learning systems. *Organization*, 7 (2), 225–46.

Zembylas, M. (2004). The emotional characteristics of teaching: an enthnographic study of one teacher. *Teaching and Teacher Education*, 20, 185–201.

11 Formation of ESL teacher identity during the first year: an introspective study

Alix Furness

Introduction

The general purpose of this chapter is to explore the formation of English as a Second Language (ESL) teacher identity through an introspective study. I approached this project with the idea that the identities of teachers of ESL must develop in a different way from identities of elementary or secondary school teachers, which has been the focus of much of the research thus far. I had been interested in learning about the development of ESL teacher identity, particularly of ESL teachers who began their teaching experience working abroad, but could find no information about it. Therefore, I decided to create my own research project, using an easily available source, myself, as a subject, and my journals as the source of data. In this introspective study, the data were collected from journals kept on a daily basis during my first year teaching junior high school in Japan. Using the journal entries, I traced my progression from a novice, visiting foreign teacher to a more practised teacher, in fact, to one who somewhat unexpectedly decided to continue teaching after returning home. I expected to see patterns of development in the personal journals I kept, but did not anticipate that these patterns would align with standard theories of teacher identity development.

Through my experiences, I grew to believe that relationships between mentors, colleagues, students, and novice teachers can often be complicated by cross-cultural misunderstandings. As I began my research, I wondered if it could be the case that the elements of teacher identity development that I thought were exclusive to my status as a foreign and temporary teacher are actually common for new teachers in general. I wondered whether cross-cultural factors complicate things, and how many of the basic steps of teacher identity development remain the same regardless of where and how the novice teacher's identity first takes shape. What I suspected as I began my research was that many of the elements that went into the development of my teacher identity would not be elements that were common to most novice teachers, because of the fact that I formed my image of myself as a teacher under teaching circumstances that are not the norm for most other new ESL teachers.

Teacher identity is something that develops gradually over time as a teacher's own education and later teaching experiences begin to accumulate. Thus teacher identity really never stops forming or changing (Bullough 1989; Fottland 2004). However, there are few studies that focus specifically on the formation of language teacher identity. There are many studies that focus on novice teachers' idealism (Palmer 1998; Hatton 2005; Marsh 2002), but not many studies on teachers who begin their teaching careers working in foreign countries, and that analyse the motivation behind embarking on such a journey that can lead to the special circumstances those overseas experiences can create. Another important issue in the development of teacher identity in the early years of teaching is the relationship between a novice teacher and her more experienced colleagues. It is important for novice teachers to have mentors, for help with both professional and personal development. There is a delicate balance that must be struck between a mentor offering support, advice and encouragement, while at the same time respecting the new teacher's authority and autonomy (Weber, 1995; Kridel *et al*, 1996). It also frequently happens that a teacher who has been assigned the role of mentor does not relish the role, and performs the function reluctantly or not at all (Bullough, 1989). However, not much research has focused on the impact of a mentor and novice ESL teachers who come from different cultural backgrounds, with different educational backgrounds, and training. In addition, there is also a gap in research that provides an introspective perspective into a new teacher's emotional and professional development. The remainder of this chapter outlines my experiences as a new teacher in Japan.

Forming teacher identity in Japan

Overall, I spent three years in Japan while living in two small towns. There was a national curriculum that the Japanese teachers were required to follow, and this did not allow for much creativity on the part of the teacher. I team-taught with a few different Japanese teachers in each of my schools, and thus I had to learn how to work with each of their different teaching styles. Some of these teachers were prepared for and enthusiastic about teaching with me, but others were not. The level of their prep and enthusiasm had a corresponding effect on my attitude towards my teaching and myself. As a novice and insecure ESL teacher, my assigned Japanese mentors' level of interest in working with me greatly influenced my image of myself as a competent teacher; the more interest they had in collaborating with me, the more worthy of the position of teacher I felt. Because I was trying not to express to my Japanese colleagues how insecure I felt at that time, I decided to express all of my doubts about my worth as a novice teacher in my teaching journals. However, at the time of writing in these journals, I never really intended to share any of the information in them, and so they provide a totally honest view of my emotional journey through my first year teaching. I wrote daily in my journal and later as I read each of the journals, I extracted the entries that pertained to my thoughts about who I was and who I wanted to be as a teacher, my feelings about my students and colleagues, and the general circumstances under which I taught, including the culture of the country in which I was living and the particular schools in which I taught during my first year. Overall, I accumulated more than 30 single-spaced pages from the journals.

Certain themes emerged repeatedly when I analysed my journals, and the six main themes that emerged were:

- Frustration, exclusion and nervousness;

- Passivity and boredom;

- Survival;

- Interaction with students;

- Interaction with colleagues; and

- Gaining confidence and knowledge.

Frustration, exclusion and nervousness

Some early themes that are evident even on day one are frustration, such as waiting to be told where to go and what to do, as well as how well I performed when I did have a task, as I assumed that I was being deliberately excluded when I was not given a brief on every aspect of that day's plan. As Bullough's (1989) research has discovered, though, frustration and feelings of being excluded are common to first-year teachers. I was not being excluded just because I was a foreigner, as I suspected at the time. The only task I had that first day was to make a speech introducing myself to the school at assembly. I was so nervous that I have no memory of making the speech. The speech was in Japanese, which I didn't speak at the time. I wrote it in English, asked a colleague to translate it, and then learned it phonetically in Japanese. I was really wanted to do well, but at the same time, I was almost hostile about the fact that no one told me what was going on that day. As far as my speech went, I had no concept of how it was received since, as I wrote in my journal, 'I don't really even remember doing it, but everyone told me I did well'.

On day two, I had already been given a couple concrete tasks like writing dialogues for a class and helping to judge a recitation contest. I wrote in my journal, 'It was really nice to be able to do some actual work for a change … it is just nice to be of use' even though the thought that I was not being of any use now seems like too early a judgement to make. During these early days the feeling of exclusion overlapped with the my feeling of frustration frequently. Although there is a general sense among novice teachers that no one tells them about what is going on in the school (Bullough 1989; Fottland 2004), much of the time in fact it is simply that the teachers who have been with or at a school long enough to know the common routines that everyone else takes for granted. However, being the only foreign teacher in my schools made it easy to for me to assume that the reason I was sometimes excluded was because I was not from the same culture as everyone else. It took much later for me to discover that this experience was not necessarily culture-based, but something teachers everywhere often complain of in their first year at a school.

Later in the first week, I note that I wrote about a special day at school, Parents Day, a day when parents visited classes. I did a lot of self-introduction lessons that day, and it was the first time I was in front of a class by myself. I felt better about my place in the school after that day because I was very active, I prepared the introductions, activities and visual aids myself, and the lesson was well-received. However, although Parents Day was successful, after a few days passed between classes, I became nervous again about the day-to-day teaching. I tried to convince myself that 'stage fright' was normal:

> I'm getting nervous again for school. I feel like it's been so long
> since (Parents' Day). I'm not going to be able to do it tomorrow.
> Which is dumb – the hardest part is over … I did my self-intro … in
> front of parents, and I did well. I know I can do it and do it under
> pressure, so I should relax. But I hear that even teachers with tons
> of experience get stage fright sometimes.

This 'stage fright' and nervousness are common for teachers no matter how much experience they have, but it is said to be most common for first year teachers to think that it is happening only because of their lack of experience, and that it will disappear with time. However, when I examined my journals from year one of teaching all the way through until today, I can see that it is still happening to me, even after more than a decade of acquiring experience.

Passivity and boredom

The first time I was unexpectedly left alone in the classroom, I did not immediately realise that the students would probably not understand my questions. Twenty days later, after a little more time in the classroom, I wrote in my journal: 'Maybe I should start writing on the board "Do you like …?" "Do you have …?" etc., so they'd all have a "guide" if they got stuck thinking of questions (for me).' It seemed as if, through trial and error rather than instruction, I was slowly beginning to figure it out. But mostly at that time I seemed passive, wanting and waiting for people to tell me what to do in and for class, and not sure of what my role was supposed to be. I often wished classes would get cancelled rather than me having to do more self introductions. However, rather than changing the introduction and activities enough to keep myself interested, or figuring out other ways to express myself or make myself useful in school, I took a passive approach, shifting between either wanting to avoid the lessons altogether or just do them as quickly as possible.

In addition to this passivity, I was bored (and later frustrated) when I wasn't sure what I should be doing, when I didn't have a set task in front of me, or when I was teaching the same lesson over and over again. I thought that this was something that was exclusive to my situation as a foreign teacher, one without my 'own' classes, but, I later discovered that other educational research has showed (e.g., Bullough 1989; Fottland 2004) that this is common for many new teachers.

Survival

One week into teaching, I was still doing self-introductions in all of my classes, so each class was virtually identical to the last one. However, one day my colleague went to the teacher's room in the middle of our class for several minutes, and I was left on my own in front of the students for the first time. I had finished my introduction, and had not prepared a plan to keep the students busy. I used this unexpected solo time to engage the students in a greeting activity I made up on the spot. I wrote in my journal, 'The other teacher forgot some worksheets and had to go get them so she asked me to keep the class busy. I stood up there, not knowing what to do, and said "Any questions about me, my family, Seattle, America?" Not much of a response.' Frightened as I was to be left alone with them, and frightened by the silence that followed my questions, I quickly deduced that I needed to stop asking questions they couldn't understand and start a very simple activity of practising handshakes and making eye contact. The mostly physical activity went well, and I survived. I seemed to be in this survival stage for a few months, but whenever I was depending on other teachers to tell me what to do in the classroom (which was most of the time during my first few months), I felt no need to 'survive' on my own. Instead, I would simply lean on my colleagues.

Interaction with students

In the third and fourth weeks of teaching I noticed that I enjoyed spending time with the students. It may seem obvious that any teacher should enjoy spending time with students. However, my focus at the beginning of my time in Japan was so much on myself, how I was feeling about being in a new country, speaking a new language, starting in a new profession, and what people's impressions of me were, that the realisation that I was happiest after quality interaction with students took me slightly by surprise. A benefit of becoming less self-centred was that I started to spend more time trying to improve my teaching, and making my contact with the students more meaningful, rather than most of my energy going towards simply surviving each individual class. The influence of those student relationships on my self-image was enormous. This could be because, as a teacher living and working so far from home, my support network was very small, and the schools where I worked became more important to me socially as well as professionally. When I became less interested in myself and more interested in my students, I felt better about whom I was as a teacher, and it seems to have been reflected in the quality of the classes I helped teach.

Interaction with colleagues

I began analysing the different teachers' teaching and classroom management techniques after about two weeks of teaching. I taught with four of them at each of my two schools, and they all had different teaching styles. I was critical of some teachers, while at the same time seemed to want to pattern myself after other teachers I admired such as the teachers who did not 'take any crap', as I wrote in my journal and harshly judged the ones who as I wrote in my journal, 'let the kids walk all over them'. Unfortunately, though, while I eventually built good relationships with my colleagues in my first year, I never had a mentor assigned to me during that first year and on reflection, I think this would have been a great help. As I became more confident about my teaching, I started feeling more qualified to draw conclusions about other teachers' performances though. I was often too critical though, and I believe it was because of my frustration at not being able to plan a class without consulting the main teacher first.

Gaining confidence and knowledge

The further I got into my first year, the more confident I felt about asking if I could plan lessons by myself and ultimately teach them too. Instead of simply trying to stay out of the way, like I did at first, I began to take on extra work and tried to help my colleagues without needing to be asked. In my first days of teaching, I seemed to think that my presence in the classroom was enough for the students to learn English. This of course shows my lack of knowledge both of teaching and of the process of learning a foreign language. For me, it would have been helpful if I had had more teacher training before going into the classroom, but it would have helped even more to know something about the development of teacher identity for first year teachers. I would have been far more relaxed had I known how many of the struggles I was experiencing were in fact as I later came to know, common for new teachers in general, and not just teachers who were living and working in foreign countries. Knowing that gradual accumulation of experience could have lessened the anxiety and depression I felt at the beginning of my first year would have assisted me in getting through that professional and cultural adjustment. When one is struggling, personally or professionally, simply knowing how normal your emotions are helps a lot with the coping process.

Conclusion

Writing a teaching journal was very important to my survival during my first year as an ESL teacher in Japan because I was able to find themes and categories that ran through my first year of teaching journal such as *Frustration, exclusion and nervousness, Passivity and boredom, Survival, Interaction with students, Interaction with colleagues,* and *Gaining confidence and knowledge.* Although none of the categories overtly refer to culture, the categories are nonetheless often centred around culture (the feelings of exclusion I had in Japan, and my relationships with colleagues and students being more important because of my being so far from home). That said however, the overarching issues behind teacher identity formation during the first year appear to be the same regardless of where and when the novice teacher starts practising the profession. Although relationships between colleagues, students, and novice teachers initially seemed to be complicated by the strains of cross-cultural communication, I found that development of teacher identity works in similar ways regardless of whether or not it happens in a cross-cultural environment, and despite what the primary motivation was behind beginning a teaching career. Elements of my teacher identity development that I thought were exclusive to my foreign status are actually common for many new teachers. Cross-cultural factors add an extra element to novice teacher self-image, but the basic steps of teacher identity development remain much the same.

References

Bullough, R. V. J. (1989). *First-year Teacher: A Case Study.* New York: Teachers College Press.

Fottland, H. (2004). Memories of a fledgling teacher: a beginning teacher's autobiography. *Teachers and Teaching: theory and practice,* 10 (6). Retrieved 15 April 2006, from: http://journalsonline.tandf.co.uk/(f4ev3i45ozlpw445jev 32m55)/app/home/contribution.asp?referrer=parent&backto=issue,4,6; journal,9,27;linkingpublicationresults,1:104807,1

Hatton, S. D. (2005). *Teaching by Heart: The Foxfire Interviews*. New York: Teacher's College Press.

Kridel, D., Bullough, R. V. J. and Shaker, P. (1996). *Teachers and Mentors: Profiles of Distinguished Twentieth-century Professors of Education*. New York: Garland Publishing.

Marsh, M. M. (2002). *The Social Fashioning of Teacher Identities*. New York: Peter Lang.

Weber, L. (1995). Reexaminations: What is the teacher and what is teaching? In W. Ayers (Ed.), *To Become a Teacher: Making a Difference in Children's Lives*. (pp. 127–61) New York: Teacher's College Press.

12 My first year of language teaching in Japan

Yukie Iwamura

Introduction

In my 19 years of teaching, I have experienced two major 'transitions' from a teacher education programme to actual teaching in a classroom. The first transition took place when I became a public junior high school teacher after graduating from a university in Japan, and the second one was when I started to teach preschool and elementary school children at a private English conversation school also in Japan. Currently, I am studying TESOL at Temple University, Japan Campus (TUJ) and preparing myself for my future teaching at a university, which will be my third transition.

As my teaching context has differed greatly from one transition to another, especially in students' age groups, each time I have felt myself being a novice teacher, with different kinds of challenges. When I compare the three, however, the extent to which I was (and will be) unprepared seems to vary depending on such factors as my knowledge of TESOL relevant to the teaching context and my prior experience applicable to the new kind of teaching. In this sense, I was least prepared in my second transition. In this article, I will describe my first two transitions in terms of the teacher education I received, the teaching context, the problems I was faced with, and how I tried to solve these problems. Then I will compare these two transitions. Next, I will describe how my current graduate studies at TUJ are preparing me for my third transition, and I will predict what kinds of problems I may encounter in this transition. I use Farrell's (2006) story structure framework to outline some of the problems I encountered and the solutions I followed (see Chapter 4 for more details on this framework).

My first transition

English teacher education

When I majored in English literature at a Japanese university, I took courses in education in order to get an English teacher's licence for junior and senior high schools in Japan. One of these courses was specifically designed to give us knowledge about teaching English. According to my incomplete lecture notes for this course, the course seemed to focus on theories and techniques relevant to teaching English at Japanese junior and senior high schools, rather than broadly cover areas in TESOL. The course content included an outline of the Course of Study for Foreign Languages issued by the Japanese Ministry of Education, a brief coverage of relevant theories of second language acquisition, how to write lesson plans, and step-by-step procedures and techniques for teaching English at junior and senior high schools in Japan based on textbooks authorised by the Ministry of Education.

As may have been natural when I took this course in the beginning of the 1980s, the professor emphasised the importance of habit formation, rather than the communicative approach. However, he also pointed out that habit formation alone will not enable learners to use the target language in real-life situations; therefore, the teacher and the learner should make efforts to create actual situations for the learner to use the language.

Another undergraduate course which prepared me to teach English was a two-week practicum at a public junior high school. I observed my master teacher's English classes, which were mostly first-year classes, and I taught a few sessions to one of these first-year classes myself. My master teacher's teaching was form-focused, and I followed his style of teaching in my lessons. I do not remember much about the lessons I taught, but I do remember that the lessons basically went smoothly without any major problems. Also, in addition to the pictures accompanying the textbook, I used some pictures I had drawn myself for these lessons. Although it was time-consuming to prepare such materials, I was happy because the students liked my pictures very much. Actually, as I look back, my lessons might have gone well even if I had not used my original pictures. The students were highly motivated to learn English and well disciplined by the master teacher.

My master teacher gave me very good comments about my lessons, noting that they were very well prepared and that my pictures were especially good. However, he advised me not to spend too much time on lesson preparation because, if I became a full-time junior high school teacher, I would be too busy to do such thorough preparation for each lesson.

Teaching context

After graduating from the university, I taught at a public junior high school (i.e., the seventh to ninth grades) for four years as a full-time teacher. It was a large junior high school with a total of approximately 1,300 students, with 45 students in each class. In my first year, I taught seven second-year classes with a total of 21 class periods per week, Monday through Saturday, each of which lasted 50 minutes. The second-year curriculum included such grammatical features as past and future tenses, comparatives, superlatives, infinitives and passive voice. There was an assigned textbook to use, which was authorised by the Ministry of Education, and I referred to model lesson plans provided in the accompanying teacher's manual in order to prepare for my lessons. Thus, the focus of this teaching involved a structural syllabus. As my master teacher in the practicum had warned me, I was too busy to prepare thoroughly for each lesson, especially in the first few months. I sometimes walked into the classroom with just the textbook and a few notes of my roughly designed lesson plan.

At that time, second-year English classes were generally harder to teach than the first- and third-year classes in junior high school. Many first-year students were highly motivated to learn English, at least in the first few months of the school year, as it was their first time to study a foreign language. However, by the time they became second-year students, many of them had lost their initial enthusiasm for studying English. Also, by that time, there was already a wide gap among students in their levels of performance. (Moreover, second-year students, who had just become teenagers, were sometimes much harder to handle than more innocent first-year students.) Third-year students, on the other hand, tended to concentrate on the lessons more than they did in the second year as most of them had to prepare for their high school entrance examinations. Thus, teaching English to the second-year students, who were neither new to English study nor pressured to study for their entrance examinations, could be more challenging than teaching the rest of the students, especially for a novice teacher. Unfortunately, I did not have a chance to practise teaching such difficult second-year classes in the practicum.

Problem

As I learned in the university that habit formation was essential in second language learning, I tried to incorporate drills into my lesson as much as possible. For example, after introducing the target sentence orally, I implemented repetition drills. I also tried other types of drills such as substitution drills and transformation drills in the course of the lesson. However, these drills, which might have worked well for highly motivated students, were hard to implement in my classes. Although my university professor said students should repeat 'clearly, loudly and rapidly' in drills, many of my students only mumbled after me; some did not even open their mouths.

As I recall, one possible reason was the fact that my students were all second-year students, whose motivation level tended to be low. Another reason might have been that the teachers who had taught my students in the previous year had probably not implemented drills in their lessons. Another more crucial reason, however, was my poor classroom management skill including that of how to discipline students. It was not easy for me to make a group of 45 students concentrate on my lesson. For example, when I was introducing the target sentence before implementing the drills, not all students looked up and listened to me: some were doing their own things, and some were even chatting with their neighbours. If the students did not understand the target sentence, there was no way they could participate in the following drills actively.

Solutions

In my first year, my classroom management skill did not improve to the extent that it could allow me to implement drills effectively. What I could do instead was to find means of compensating for my poor classroom management skill. I tried to make my lesson, especially the beginning part of my lesson, more interesting by using my original visual aids and by telling my students interesting episodes from my own English learning experience. When the students found the lesson interesting, they followed my instruction more willingly and concentrated better.

Using original visual aids

As I had used my original pictures in the practicum, I used original visual aids at this junior high school in order to make my lessons interesting. This time, however, I used an overhead projector instead of just showing pictures drawn on paper. Actually, using an overhead projector was suggested by the vice principal, who used to teach English: I had never thought of using such an equipment for English lessons. There were a few overhead projectors available in the school, and the vice principal showed me how to use them and encouraged me to use one in my English lessons. After that, I often used an overhead projector in my oral introduction of the target sentence. For example, I made a comic strip focusing on the target sentence and showed it with an overhead projector as I introduced the sentence. (An example is shown in Figure 12.1.)

Using an overhead projector had some advantages over using pictures drawn on paper. For example, as the screen was almost as big as the blackboard (and my comic strip was funny), all the students looked up and listened to my oral introduction carefully. Thus, more students understood the target sentence than before. Also, as my comic strip made my students laugh, this helped them speak clearly, loudly and rapidly during the immediately following repetition drills, at least for a short time. Another advantage of using an overhead projector was that it took less time to draw pictures on sheets for overhead projectors than to draw large pictures on paper. Thus, although it was still not easy, I somehow managed to make original visual aids in my busy schedule.

Actually, the idea of utilizing original visual aids came from my past experience as a Sunday school teacher although I was not conscious of this when I was teaching at the junior high school. I was a Sunday school teacher at a local Christian church for a few years when I was a university student. When I told bible-related stories to elementary school students (in Japanese) in Sunday school, I often used visual aids, such

Figure 12.1. A comic strip presenting the target sentence 'I saw a ghost'.

as ready-made paper plays and my originally created ones. These visual aids, especially my original ones, attracted students' attention and made my story-telling interesting although I was not as good a story-teller as veteran teachers. From this experience, I learned that well-prepared visual aids could compensate for a lack of teaching experience. This experience influenced my decisions about how to solve my problem at the junior high school.

Telling episodes from my own English learning experience

Another thing I tried was to tell my students in Japanese some interesting episodes of my English learning experience. For example, I told my students a story such as this: 'When I was a university student, an American woman asked me at a train station, "Is there a rest room here?" After a moment's thought, I said, "No. But there is a bench over there." As she looked confused, I continued, "You can sit down and take a rest." Then, she said, "No, no. What I mean is a toilet!" I was not sure what a rest room meant, so I guessed it was a room where people take a rest, but I was wrong!' A short story like this added spice to my lesson and helped the students concentrate on the following activity. Actually, I wanted to tell these episodes in English because I learned at the university that teachers should try to use English as much as possible in class. In fact, at first I tried to tell my episodes in English. However, some students started chatting because they could not understand the story. Telling an episode concisely in the students' L1 was much more effective than spending much time explaining it in very simple English, which still could not be understood by half of the students and encouraged them to be noisy. I began to believe that the purposeful and well-calculated use of the students' L1, especially in the beginners' classes, could actually promote students' learning and aid the teacher.

During my four years of teaching at the public junior high school, I became aware of its limitations as a place for students to learn English effectively as well as a place for me to develop myself as a teacher. There seemed to be too many constraints for ideal English education to take place in such an environment, with factors such as large, multi-level classes, a pre-determined curriculum in textbooks authorised by the Ministry of Education, and high school entrance examinations which made it difficult for teachers to spend time on more practical English. Also, I wanted to try a different kind of teaching other than habit formation in a different teaching environment, all of which made me decide to work for a private English conversation school whose goal was to teach English for communication.

My second transition

Teaching context

The second school I worked at was a private English conversation school with several branches, whose students ranged in age from two years to adults. In my first year, I was assigned to the children's division and taught preschool and elementary school students' classes. Among them, the one which gave me the biggest 'reality shock' was the two-year-old students' class, so I will focus my discussion only on this class. Teaching English to two-year-old babies was such a different experience from my previous teaching that I could not apply any of my assumptions about teaching or techniques I had used before.

There were about ten students in this class, who were all two years old and still learning to speak their first language, Japanese. They were all new students who had never been in an English speaking environment. The course met once a week for 80 minutes which included about 20 minutes' snack time. I was the main teacher, and there was one assistant who helped me take care of the students and modelled short dialogues with me. The school allowed the students' parents to stay in the classroom until they felt their children were ready to attend the lessons on their own. In my class, there were always a few parents in the classroom in my first year.

My teaching context at this school was very different from that at the previous school. In this school, at least in my first year, the teachers had much freedom in deciding class content. There was no textbook or teacher's manual to follow but just a list of words, phrases, and songs to cover in each term. The classroom was very different as well. There were no desks and chairs but one or two long movable tables and enough stools for every student to sit, which were rarely used because we basically implemented techniques that made the students move a lot or sit on the floor. The classroom was rather spacious for a language class as it was actually a room for dance lessons.

Teacher training

I do not have any written records of the training I received, but I remember that the pre-service training content included the school's basic principles of teaching and some useful techniques for teaching different age groups of children. As it was not an academic training programme like the one I had received at my university, it focused on practical issues rather than theories related to children's second language acquisition. Nonetheless, I was excited to try a totally different kind of teaching to students much younger than the junior high school students I used to teach. In addition to receiving the pre-service training, I assisted a veteran teacher in her three-year-old students' class for one year. This turned out to be the most useful training for me because I was able to learn what to teach and how to teach it from her every week, most of which I used in my following week's lesson plan. Actually, without this kind of training, it would have been impossible for me to survive my first year because the school did not provide teachers with a detailed syllabus or a teacher's manual.

I was always fascinated by the way my master teacher taught her class. Her teaching was like an art. Her lesson plans were not detailed but had only points to cover in the day's lesson, and she proceeded from one activity to another smoothly with no hustle or extra energy, speaking mostly in English. She rarely needed to shout to discipline her students. The minute she started to do something, the students were attracted to her as if she were a magnet. In her class, students acted out words and songs, played train and store, drew pictures, and learned to speak simple English words and phrases naturally. Although her students were all new students, it did not take long until all their parents left the classroom.

Problem

I wished to lead my class as my master teacher did. However, even though I tried to implement the techniques I learned from her in the way she did, they did not work in my class. I could not organize my class of ten two-year-old babies. When I started to do an activity, some students would join me, but one or two would be running around in the spacious classroom, one or two would be sitting with her mother, and one or two would be doing his own thing in a corner of the classroom. Often there were a few latecomers. Every time someone came late, some students would run to the door to find out who he or she was. In this kind of situation, the students did not make much progress in speaking English. When there had been a classroom management problem in the junior high school, I had often discussed it with the students in Japanese. However, this was not possible with these two-year-old babies who could not have such a discussion. Also, I hesitated to speak much Japanese to them because there were always a few parents in the classroom who might think I was neglecting my job.

Actually, what puzzled me most was the fact that I could not analyse my problem very well. I was not really sure where my real problem was: classroom management, students' motivation, lesson planning, techniques, or whatever. As a result, I could not take a focused approach to solving my problem as I had done at the junior high school. This situation did not improve much in my first year, which frustrated me and gradually made me lose confidence in teaching. (Even when the students somehow started to settle down, a new student or someone for a trial lesson came, then the class lost its order again.)

Solutions

In the beginning of my second year of teaching this same class (which included two- and three-year old students), I was given hints by the school's chairperson, which helped me improve my situation. As part of the teacher training programme, she observed my class and gave me useful comments. To my surprise, her first piece of advice was to implement the lesson without the students' parents. She said that the students were all ready to attend the class on their own and that they would not pay full attention to me and my assistant if someone's parent was in the classroom. She even talked to each parent who was still staying in the classroom to persuade them to leave the classroom. Another useful piece of advice from her was to change the pacing of my lessons. She said I should conduct the lessons faster so that I could keep the students' interest and not allow any uncontrolled moments in which students would spread out.

Lesson without the students' parents

I followed the chairperson's advice and started to implement lessons without the students' parents. For the first two weeks (i.e. two sessions) all the students kept crying furiously for almost 80 minutes. However, during the third session, there was an incident which dramatically changed the class atmosphere. In this session, although they were all crying in the beginning, the students seemed to get tired of crying after 30 minutes or so. Then a girl started playing with a stool: Just like going through a small tunnel, she crawled under the four-legged stool. This caught some students' attention, and they started to do the same. Also, my assistant and I helped the other students do the same. Then, in a matter of a few minutes, the classroom started to echo with all the students' laughter. During this time, I did not hesitate to speak to them in Japanese because I thought making them feel unthreatened and comfortable would be more important than making them learn English at that moment. After the lesson, when the students' parents came to pick up their children, they looked relieved to see their children's smiling faces.

From this session on, it became much easier for me to teach this class. The students did not cry even though their parents did not stay in the classroom. Apparently, both the students and I felt much more comfortable being together than before, and the students' parents seemed to have more trust in me. Furthermore, although it was still not easy, somehow I was able to organise the classes and implement my lesson plans. To my surprise, when those students who had always been with their parents started to participate in activities, they were able to say the words and phrases I had taught before. Obviously, they had been listening to the lessons and had been receiving a lot of input in this way.

This experience taught me a few important lessons. First, I realised that teaching should be something that the teacher and the students create together through interaction, rather than the teacher executing pre-planned lessons one-sidedly. This was what I could never learn at the junior high school. We learn a lot from our students. In fact, until the girl in my class showed me, I did not know that two-year-old students would enjoy such a simple activity as crawling under a stool. What I had been trying to do was perhaps too advanced for their age. As my master teacher's students were several months older than my students, activities which worked in her class may have been too difficult for my students.

Doing the lesson with only my assistant and the students allowed me to have more leeway to observe my students without being conscious of the parents' eyes. Also, it allowed me to try different techniques with my students and to find out what they liked to do, by trial and error. These were actually part of a necessary process that a novice teacher should go through in order to learn to teach, but I could not do that because I was always conscious of the parents' eyes. Perhaps such parents' eyes would not affect a veteran teacher so much, but apparently they did greatly affect a novice teacher like me.

Another discovery was that, especially when teaching small children, we should give the highest priority to establishing a good rapport with the students (and their parents) at an early stage. My master teacher, with her long teaching experience and confidence, was able to make her students feel comfortable the minute they entered the classroom even though speaking to them mostly in English. (This was why her students' parents decided to leave the classroom soon.) In my case, however, it took a long time to establish a trusting relationship with my students and their parents. This eventually led to delayed progress of my students' English performance. Therefore, establishing a good relationship with the students at an early stage is extremely important. Even if this involves a little use of the students' native language by a novice teacher, it is justifiable.

Changing the pacing of the lesson

Another suggestion the chairperson made for me was to pace my lesson faster. For this purpose, I tried to spend more time on lesson planning in order to include more activities than before, including backup activities in case some did not work. Also, as the chairperson suggested, I tried to make the transition smooth from one activity to another so that the students would not spread out while I was preparing for the next activity. This required thorough preparation of props before the lesson started and a detailed meeting with my assistant so that she could prepare the props for the next activity while I was doing one activity with the students. Although it took time, these efforts did pay off, and gradually the class started to settle down.

My master teacher paced her lesson rather slowly, at least it seemed to me, and she never did anything in haste, and still her class always went smoothly and was lively. Even when her props were not well prepared, she could make the transition smooth by, for example, making the students help her prepare the props as part of an activity, or by preparing the props in a fun way in front of the students so that the students would enjoy watching her. What made it possible for her to do these things might be partly her long experience in teaching small children and partly her inborn talent or something that could not be explained. Obviously, her elegant, slow-paced style of teaching was something I could not imitate as a novice teacher, at least in the two-year-old babies' class, although I wished to. As a strategy to compensate for this, I needed to pace my lesson faster with thorough preparation, which helped me survive my first years of teaching babies. I do not know if longer experience could have made it possible for me to teach a group of ten two-year-old babies in such an elegant manner as my master teacher's. Unfortunately, I never had a chance to teach such young babies' classes again after the first few years as I mostly taught elementary school students in later years.

Comparing my first and second transitions

When I look back, my second transition was much more challenging than my first transition: I felt it was much harder for me to adjust myself to the new teaching environment in the second transition than in the first. I can think of two main factors. One is the extent to which the environment allowed me to learn to teach by trial and error and to generalise characteristics of specific age groups of students. Partly, this depended on how many times I could teach the same course content to different groups of students and how many students of the same age group I could teach in my first year. In this sense, I was in an ideal situation at the first school.

At the first junior high school, I taught seven second-year classes in my first year. This means that I taught the same lesson to seven different groups of students each week and in one year. This allowed me to try different ways of teaching so that I could figure out what worked and what did not as well as find out how one activity which worked well for one group of students could not for another group. Also, as each class consisted of 45 students, I taught a total of more than 300 students of the same age group and met them three times a week. This made it possible for me to find out characteristics of this particular age group of students with relative ease.

At the second school, however, my situation was far from ideal. As I was a full-time staff member and had many things to do besides teaching, I could not teach many classes. Also, I taught different class content to different age groups of students. As a result, I had only one or two chances to teach the same course content each week and in one year. This, compared to seven chances at the junior high school, was not adequate in order to learn to teach by trial and error. Furthermore, I taught only about ten or fewer students of the same age group at the second school, which, compared with over 300 at the first school, was not enough to allow me to generalise characteristics of a particular age group of students in one year.

The second (and more important) factor which made my adjustment harder at the second school was that I did not have any academic knowledge relevant to teaching very young learners. Neither the teacher education programme at my university nor the one at the conversation school provided me with such knowledge. When I was teaching at the junior high school, I was able to analyse my problem within the framework of the habit formation theory. Although it is labelled as an incomplete theory now, the habit formation theory at least gave me some direction in thinking how I could improve my teaching at that time. Because of this, I was able to tackle my problem with a positive attitude. However, in my second transition, I could not take such a positive attitude. I was completely lost and could not figure out what my problem was by myself until the chairperson helped me. I even wondered why I was teaching such young learners. As I could not find a goal of my teaching, I felt as if I were walking in a dark tunnel without knowing where I was headed. What could have helped me cope with such a situation, however, was some academic knowledge relevant to my new teaching context. For example, had I been familiar with the 'Critical Period Hypothesis' and the various debates about this hypothesis (or 'maturational constraints in second-language acquisition'), it would have given me more of a focused reason for my teaching two-year-old babies. At least, I would have appreciated it as an opportunity to ponder over the validity of the hypothesis myself. Also, if I had known about the 'silent period', I would not have worried unduly about my inability to make my students speak English sooner. Instead, I could have set my goal first on exposing them to a lot of English. Actually, trying to make each student speak not only required a lot of extra energy but also slowed down the pacing of my lesson, so just shifting my initial goal from making them speak English to giving them a lot of English input might have made my teaching a lot easier.

My third transition

Teacher education

I am currently studying TESOL at TUJ in order to update my knowledge of theories and techniques in TESOL. I wish to get a teaching position at a university after graduation; thus, I am now preparing myself for my third transition. My newly gained knowledge includes updated first and second language acquisition theories, current approaches to language teaching such as Content-Based Instruction and Task-Based Language Teaching, classroom techniques based on current understanding of second language acquisition, and issues related to TESOL.

Among the things I learned at TUJ, what surprised me most was the current notion of the 'post-methods era'. As my teaching career started with my belief in habit formation, or the Audiolingual Method, and my quest for a better method actually led my journey as a language teacher, the notion of the post-methods era gave me a new perspective on language teaching. I learned that, rather than look for all answers from one method or a set of methodologies proposed by others, I should keep myself updated with findings and issues about TESOL and make informed decisions about teaching based on my own developing theories of teaching and learning a second language. TUJ has empowered me by providing me with ways of keeping myself updated with such knowledge, such as from literature, as well as ways of finding solutions to classroom problems on my own, such as by action research. In addition to gaining knowledge about teaching, I had a chance to take a practicum at TUJ, in which I observed an undergraduate writing course for one semester and taught one session myself. This experience gave me some picture of what I should expect if I start teaching at a university. Based on this experience, I can predict what kinds of problems I might face when I start teaching undergraduate students.

Predictable problems

I can think of two problems I may encounter when I start teaching at a university. One is related to techniques. I have almost no repertoire of techniques suitable for students at the university level. When I taught an undergraduate class in the practicum, I realised none of the techniques I had used with children were usable in teaching university students. In this sense I may have to start almost from scratch if I get a teaching position at a university. Another problem may be that I know very few materials suitable for university courses. This can be a problem if I have to choose a textbook by myself. It seems to me that using materials suitable for students both in terms of the content and the level of English can be one key factor to make the lesson interesting and meaningful. If I make a wrong choice of materials, it will be extremely hard for me, with my lack of experience in teaching university students, to keep the students interested and active in class.

Besides these problems related to techniques and materials, I cannot predict any major problems at present. Some of the problems I was faced with at the previous schools, such as those of classroom management, lesson planning, and the pacing of the lesson, may not be big problems any more. At least, I thought so when I taught undergraduate students in the practicum. It seems that the basic skills of teaching I attained in these areas in my past teaching are applicable to teaching university students.

Also, I can predict that the biggest problem I had in my second transition can be avoided. What agonised me most when teaching two-year-old students was the sense of lack of direction, even of helplessness, rather than technical problems in themselves. TUJ has empowered me with academic knowledge so that I could cope with my new challenge positively. For example, my knowledge of categories of inquiry in TESOL as well as current theories and controversies in those categories can help me analyse my situation when I encounter a problem. Furthermore, my graduate studies have trained me to search for answers from literature in TESOL, and they also have informed me of action research. Thus, I am now equipped with some ways of finding solutions to my problems, which of course do not guarantee me appropriate solutions to such problems but at least would give me some hints for improvement.

Reflections

Reflecting upon my transitions, I have reached the following realisation: although teacher education programmes cannot prepare new teachers for every possible teaching context, they may be able to equip the teachers with ways of tackling their future problems proactively. For example, giving them some prior knowledge about problems they may encounter may help, such as the ideas presented in this book. Also, some academic knowledge about techniques to analyse their problematic situation and some ways of finding solutions may be useful. Novice teachers may benefit from using some strategies to compensate for their lack of experience and teaching skills. In my case, for example, using visual aids and purposeful use of students' L1 helped me survive my first transition, and faster pacing of lessons helped me in my second transition. Therefore, it may be useful to suggest some strategies of this kind in teacher education because novice teachers cannot expect to reach the level of experienced teachers in their teaching skills within a short time.

References

Farrell, T. S. C. (2006). The first year of language teaching: imposing order. *System, 34*, 211–21.

CPSIA information can be obtained
at www.ICGtesting.com
Printed in the USA
BVHW090900070219
539590BV00006B/14/P